COST EFFECTIVENESS OF HIGHER EDUCATION

About the Author

Dr. M.M. Ansari is on the staff of Economic and Scientific Research Foundation, New Delhi. He holds a Doctoral Degree in Economics, obtained his Master's degree (Eco.) in First Division, and Post-Graduate Diploma in Public Finance (U.K.). He was Joint Director and Head of Research Cell in Economics of Education, AIU (1985-1994), Fellow, NIEPA (1984-85) and Consultant, Planning Commission (1981-84). He has been Consultant to various national and international organisations. He has served as Expert on Educational Planning and Finance for ADB's Technical Assistance Project on HRD in Micronesia (1994-95); and Bihar Education Project (1995-96). He is the author of several books/monographs (15) and papers/articles (80) in professional journals. His books and monographs include among others. *Resource Mobilisation by Universities* (Spellbound) 1997; *Human Resource Development in Micronesia,* Vol. I & II (Co-author) (ADB/IRD) 1995; *Fiscal Policy for University Development*, (Concept) 1994; *Economics of Distance Higher Education* (Concept) 1992; *University-Industry Interaction*, 1990; *Studies in Distance Education* (Co-ed.) (IGNOU) 1988; *Education and Economic Development* 1987; and *Tax Ratio and Tax Effort Analysis*, UCB, 1980. His areas of specialisation are Economics of Education and Public Finance.

COST EFFECTIVENESS OF HIGHER EDUCATION

A Critical Assessment

M.M. ANSARI

Foreword by

J.L. AZAD

CONCEPT PUBLISHING COMPANY, NEW DELHI - 110059

ISBN 81-7022-540-X

First Published 1997

Published and Printed by

Ashok Kumar Mittal
Concept Publishing Company
A/15-16, Commercial Block, Mohan Garden,
NEW DELHI - 110059 (India)

Phones: 5554042, 5504042
Fax No. 091-11-5598898

FOREWORD

Educational finance, as an area of research has, in the recent past, attracted attention of academics and researchers. A number of studies on various aspects of educational finance, particularly at the higher education stage, have been conducted. Most of these studies have underscored the recurrent problems of higher education, particularly the resource constraints which has, of late, afflicted the university system. Quite a few studies have discussed the patterns of income and expenditure, procedures of grants from the Central and State Governments and the sources of finance, etc. Very few studies, have, however, analysed the allocative efficiency of the university system or the effectiveness of the large investment that is ploughed into the university system year after year.

It would be readily conceded that in order to enable the universities to discharge their twin functions of extending the frontiers of knowledge and producing competent professionals and enlightened citizens of tomorrow, they have to be given the fullest autonomy in academic matters, besides the provision of adequate financial resources for their maintenance and development. It is only in an atmosphere of academic freedom that the intellect can blossom to its fullest extent. One would, however, justifiably expect that the receipient institutions of public largesse would ensure that the heavy investment that a resource starved country like India makes in them is rationally utilised. Thus, university autonomy is to be tempered with public accountability of their performance. This would call for a scientific and objective review of the utilisation of financial inputs in the university system as well as the output generated by them. It is in this context that the study of cost effectiveness of higher education undertaken by Dr. M.M. Ansari assumes considerable significance.

The study under reference, which is confined to a cross-section of 15 universities, attempts to make a critical assessment of cost effectiveness of higher education by calculating unit costs for various types of university institutions as also for the various courses of study. The broad objectives are to assess the extent of efficiency in allocation of resources and management of funds as well as the likely effects of the university outputs on socio-economic activities. These are very laudable objectives in that not much empirical evidence is available on these aspects.

An important highlight of the study is a comprehensive analysis of the development of higher education in physical and financial terms. The phenomenal growth of student enrolment as well as institutions has been succinctly brought out. There are, however, wide difference in the distribution of institutions for various levels and types of education across the States. Similar variations have been noticed in the pattern of expenditure as also distribution of resources among different functional heads. For obvious reasons, the Central universities are more dependent on the Central Government including the Central funding agencies. The State universities, however, depend on State grants and fees, etc. Further, the revenue raising policies and practices followed by different universities vary substantially among the universities. It has also been revealed that staff salaries are the main constituent of university expenditure. A disturbing implication of the preponderance of expenditure on staff salaries is the comparative neglect of other items of expenditure like physical infrastructure, student services, etc.

There is a very interesting analysis of unit costs in different types of institutions. The study identifies two types of costs—the "raw" unit costs, which have been worked out by dividing the total expenditure by total enrolment and the "adjusted" unit costs for which a somewhat more sophisticated method has been utilised. The latter costs have been worked out by dividing the total expenditure by weighted enrolments. These weights have been assigned keeping in view the level of education and the nature of technology used for effective learning by the students.

The analysis shows wide variations in the unit costs for different types of institutions and in respect of various diciplines. The multiplicity of factors contributing to the differences in unit costs of different disciplines like variations in the pay scales of staff, differences in the nature and types of universities, etc., have been identified. The moot point, which needs further pushing is the emergence of widely disparate cost structure of discipline, having almost similar financial, physical and academic inputs. The real contribution of the study, however, lies in measuring the cost effectiveness of different academic disciplines. The analysis reveals considerable wastage of resources as measured by the students' performance at the university examinations. It has also been found that there is less emphasis on professional and technical education and a lower level of achievement with respect to academic excellence.

The study has questioned the authenticity of a number of 'myths' that have gained currency in the realm of higher education finance. For example, the evidence deduced in the study reveals that there is no systematic relationship between unit costs and student-teacher (ST) ratios. Further that low student-teacher ratios do not necessarily lead to better academic performance.

Another widely prevalent belief that university activities suffer because of resource crunch also does not find enough corroborative evidence in the study. It has been found that higher unit costs do not necessarily lead to better performance.

The study of cost effectiveness of the universities indicate a grim picture of universities performance. There is a very high incidence of wastage inspite of low ST ratios and high unit costs. Further, except for science and science based disciplines, the learning achievements of students is generally low. It is also noted that the internal and external efficiency of the university system leaves much to be desired. There is considerable mis-allocation of resources leading to serious internal inefficiency in resource utilisation. These findings are a pointer to some serious malfunctioning of the university system, which a poor country, like ours can ill-afford.

While discussing policy implication, the author has made a forceful plea for adopting a uniform approach for funding university institutions. The best method of doing this is to adopt the unit cost system as a basis for the determination of finances for universities. Admittedly, this is the most judicious and scientific method of funding university institutions. Care has, however, to be taken to work out region and discipline specific costs and to keep them under periodic review.

Another important suggestion, which emerges from the study, is the abolition of matching basis of funding, which is, presently in vogue. It has been rightly stated that this system is unscientific and leads to inequity and inefficiency in institutional management. The best way to acheive this objective is to demarcate the areas of responsibility between the Central and State Governments, keeping in view their respective Constitutional responsibilities. Under this dispensation, the Central Government should provide full funding for schemes, which are of national significance while the State Governments may fund schemes, which are local and regional in character.

Another important suggestion is to introduce a process of planned development of universities, keeping in view the requirements of various categories of professional and technical manpower as also personnel of other categories. The researcher goes further and recommends that each university should be allotted a share of number of students in relation to available infrastructure and past performance, and they should be funded on the basis of that predetermined enrolment. The Government grant calculated on that basis should be given as block grant. If an institution wants to enrol more students, it should do so as an autonomous organisation, out of its own resources.

The suggestion made by the author is worth serious consideration by the funding authorities. In England, a similar system of 'guide' prices and 'bid' system for various disciplines keeping in view the capacity of institution to cater to the pre-determined enrolment is already in vogue. We shall have to evolve a system of integrated planning in case we have to take the university institutions out of the academic morass in which most of them find themselves at present.

Another important suggestion made in the study relates to improving cost efficiency of the universities. In this context, the modification of the system of university budgeting and rationalising the expenditure on academic and infrastructural facilities has been stressed. It has also been suggested that in order to bring about uniformity in the admission of students and to effect economies in costs, common entrance tests by institutions offering similar courses should be organised. This has already been operationalised in some of professional institutions also.

Among the measures for ensuring cost effectiveness of the university system, stress has been laid on the need for enhancing cost recoveries from the students by linking them with the ever escalating costs of education. It has also been rightly emphasised that the rates of user's charges like hostel, laborataries, etc., should be objectively determined and recovered. Another useful suggestion is that the education of foreign students should not be subsidised. The need for raising resources from industrial and commercial houses has also been underscored. Another suggestion that needs implementation is the introduction of a wide range scheme of inflationary adjusted, interest free loans to needy students so as to generate a revolving and self-sustaining fund.

It is difficult to discuss the various suggestions made in the study in the short span of this preface. It may, however, be said that the study has covered the wide spectrum of university finances and highlightened some of the very important issues relating to university management systems. The author has been able to subject to the voluminous data relating to university finances to a critical analysis. The interpretation of the data has been done with a rare degree of competence and objectivity. At no point, he has allowed his own predilections to come into play. There is nothing in his statements which is not based on sound empirical evidence.

I have every hope that the study by Dr. Ansari would be a trend setter in the world of higher education finance. It will also impel the decision-makers in the Government as also the funding bodies to realise that there is something basically wrong with the present system of resource allocation for higher education and their utilisation by the institutions. Further, that the pattern and precedures of financing higher education need to be drastically overhauled so as to bring them in conformity with the fast changing needs of university institutions.

The study would also enable the universities to set their house in order before expecting the nation to invest substantial amount for their maintenance and development. While any infringement in their autonomous character is reprehensible, they have also to be accountable to the people, who have to part with their hard earned money for their sustenance and who entrust the future of their young ones to their care. In fact, the destiny of the nation is to be shaped in the haloed precincts of university institutions. It is, therefore, not too much to expect that the university institutions will come out of the shell of academic exclusiveness and become an active participant in the great task of building a stronger, resurgent India.

I would commend this study to policy-makers, academics, university administrators at the Central and State levels, and to all those concerned with the financing and administration of university education. It is also a very good reference material for the intending researchers and students, who want to understand the variegated problems of university finances and the extent of efficiency with which the resources are utilised by institutions of higher education. In fact, it is an essential reading material for all those, who genuienly wish that the working of the university system should be streamlined and the recurring problems of resource constraints should be solved for good.

March 10, 1997

J.L. Azad

PREFACE

The composition of labour force has been changing due to growth of knowledge, improvement in technology and deliberate economic policies, mainly under the aegis of structural adjustment programme, to expedite economic progress. Upgradation of human capability through concerned efforts to augment opportunities for education, training and health care is *sine qua non* for enabling the manpower to be able to function in the modern technocratic society. The factors like human development index, the average years of schooling of the working population, share of educated and skilled persons in the total labour force, gross enrolment ratio with respect to school going population are unfavourable for India as compared to the average for some of the developing countries. Urgent attention should therefore be paid to relax the constraints on augmentation of opportunities for learning, skill development and technological innovations. In this context, the role of higher education institutions (HEIs) is critical for meeting the manpower requirements of all types and levels as well as for providing direction for change in the overall system of education.

Of late, considerable efforts have been made by institutions and individuals scholar to diagnose the ills from which HEIs have been suffering. A number of prescriptive measures have also been suggested, yet there is no perceptible improvement in performance and accountability of institutions. As the level of higher education efforts, as measured by enrolment ratio (6 per cent), S&T manpower per thousand of population (3.5 persons) and allocation of resources (about 0.6 per cent of GNP) are one of the lowest in the world, it is imperative to explore the ways and measures for expanding and diversifying the programmes of higher education such that equity and efficiency criteria of funding HEIs are duly satisfied. Since resources are limited and the competing claims of various socio-economic services are high, the fiscal prudence in use of funds and performance in delivery of services will eventually determine eligibility for additional resources, particularly in the libralised economic environment. The mechanisms of financing HEIs in vogue mainly on trend basis do not entail an objective assessment of academic and financial performance or application of manpower planning approach to determine the magnitude of funds required to finance the programmes of higher education. As a result, not only the system is underfunded from the view point of qualitative and quantitative achievements, but the meagre resources allocated for the system are inefficiently utilised also. I have noted elsewhere that due to allocative inefficiency, the outcome and input of HEIs activities are not necessarily consistent with the objective of social justice and economic efficiency. This observations has indeed provided us a strong motivation to undertake a comprehensive exercise on cost-effectiveness of higher education with a view to obtaining some insight into the aspects of financial management of HEIs and to debate on various aspects of reforms contemplated by the funding agencies, mainly the Central and State government as well as the beneficiaries. I hope that this contribution will provide a fresh impetus for fiscal reforms in the management of HEIs.

I express my enormous thanks to Dr. J.L. Azad who was always very willing to discuss the problems and issues in financing higher education. His comments on an earlier version of the draft report have been very helpful in improving the content and presentation of facts. He was also kind enough to accede to my request to write the foreword to this book.

On various issues dealt with in this book, I had the privilege of receiving helpful comments and having enlightened discussions with Prof. A.M. Khusro, Shri Anand Sarup, Prof. S.K. Agrawala, Dr. P.R. Panchamukhi, Dr. J.B.G. Tilak and Dr. T.C. Sharma. I am especially grateful to Dr. Sharma who provided competent research support, particularly for Chapter 3 which deals with unit costs analysis. His vast experience and expertise in higher education research were of immense value in preparation of this document. Ms. Zeenet Shafi ably provided commendable research support in preparation of Chapter 2, which focuses on the developments in higher education. I am extremely grateful to them.

Without the cooperation of university authorities, Vice-Chancellors, Registrars and Finance Officers of various universities, especially those included in this study, it would not have been possible to undertake this research study. I am extremely indebted to them for providing the relevant documents as well as necessary feedback for improvements in empirical exercises.

I am grateful to the Concept Publishing Company for undertaking the responsibility of the publication arrangement of this book.

I need hardly add that none of the above mentioned, can be held responsible for the errors and omissions that might have still remained in the book.

April 7, 1997 M.M. ANSARI

CONTENTS

LIST OF TABLES

EXECUTIVE SUMMARY

The Issues

Increased understanding of the relationship between higher education and socio-economic progress calls for a greater attention to reform the system of planning, financing and management of higher education to ensure the realisation of such national goals as creation of an enlightened and prosperous society. The diversities in socio-economic settings and the complex nature of required developmental inputs, necessitate *inter alia* building up of solid infrastructure and preparing a cadre of manpower through high quality of relevant education and training. The perceived role of education in development has led to establishment of various types and levels of institutions having multifarious activities which are deemed crucial for human development. Inspite of commendable progress in expansion and diversification of higher education activities, the level of human capital formation as measured by number of average years of schooling (2.4 years) and proportion of age specific population attending educational institutions (50 per cent), including tertiary level, is one of the lowest as compared to other developing countries. Within the country, such differences are glaring across the regions and socio-economic groups. There is, therefore, much to be desired insofar as institutional efforts for meeting the educational needs of individuals and society are concerned. The constraints on further augmentation of opportunity for learning to meet the growing and diverse nature of higher education, training and research are required to be relaxed, particularly to ensure that the process of upgradation of knowledge and skills of manpower duly transforms the working population to enable them to function in the knowledge and technology driven economy. It would, however, require *inter alia* that planning, financing and management of institutions should be suitably modified in order that they effectively respond to the changes in the social aspirations and manpower needs of the economy especially under the aegis of structural adjustment and increasing globalisation of economy, in which low level of human capital formation or lack of competence of labour force is threatening development.

The prevailing policies on the development of higher education institutions (HEIs) and performance of HEIs with respect to both internal and external efficiency are not in tune with the national policies of raising overall efficiency in use of resources and expanding the productive capacity of the economy. A critical assessment of cost effectiveness of higher education amply substantiates the point. The approach of unit costs analysis as employed in this study lend desirable perspective on the extent of efficiency in allocation and management of funds as well as the likely effects of the university outputs on socio-economic activities. The study of a cross section of universities, fifteen (15), shed light on such crucial aspects as the pattern of resource allocation across the institutions and academic departments, efficiency in use of funds, and performance in terms of students' learning attainments. An understanding of these aspects is imperative to reform the policies and practices of financing and management of higher education system. The major findings of this study are:

Developments in Higher Education

Higher education system has continued to be exposed to greater pressures for expansion and diversification of programmes to cater for the manpower needs of economy and the society, particularly, in the context of changing socio-economic environment. The growth in institutions, enrolment and finance has recorded manifold increase during the plan periods, yet the share of educated and trained persons in the total labour force is one of the lowest for India, as compared to the average for the developing countries. The system's response to improve upon the qualitative and quantitative dimensions has, therefore, been inadequate.

A multiple of factors like financial constraints, inefficiency in use of resources, lack of academic accountability, etc., have adversely affected the development of higher education, and these factors are most likely to impinge upon the efforts to enrich human resources through education and training programmes in the foreseeable future also.

The responsibility of providing higher education services is shared between the Centre and the States, the latter being largely and traditionally responsible for financing and management of colleges and universities. The HEIs under the aegis of the Centre and the States offer different types and levels of programmes; and in the last four decades or so, the number of universities and colleges has increased seven and ten times, respectively. While there are considerable differences across the States in establishing HEIs, most institutions are established to cater for general higher education (87 per cent) rather than professional and technical education. In the regime of an already high graduate unemployment, and changing structure of productive activities as well as the composition of labour force such a direction of expansion, as above, seem unplanned and indicate misplaced emphasis for producing non-technical professional students, which also reflect allocative inefficiency in deployment of funds. In none of the States, there has been any systematic attempt to assess the different types and levels of manpower, which should be supported by the States to provide for relevant education and training. There is, therefore much to be desired insofar as sound planning and management of HEIs programmes are concerned.

The Centre has however adopted a somewhat cautious approach as its efforts are concentrated in promotion of technical and professional education since the beginning of Five Year Plans. During the period 1950-51 to 1990-91, the number of institutions and enrolment in professional institutions have, for instance, increased as many times as 12 and 8, respectively.

The overall enrolment for higher education has increased at the rate of 10 per cent per annum since 1950-51. Under graduate students account for 89 per cent whereas the share of research students is as low as 1.1 per cent. More than four-fifths of student are enrolled in affiliating colleges, mainly at undergraduate level. There is no significant shift in enrolment pattern from general higher education to professional courses. The female students account for nearly one-third of the total enrolment, the highest and lowest shares being for Kerala (53 per cent) and Bihar (16 per cent). As against the overall student-teacher ratio of 16:1 for higher education, the corresponding ratios for universities and colleges emerge to be 12 to 17 respectively, which does not indicate over crowding of the system. There is, therefore, scope for generating economies of scale and improving standard of teaching and research.

Of the total educational outlays, the expenditure on higher education in 1990-91, accounted for 13.5 per cent; the respective shares of plan and non-plan being 12 and 88 per cent. More than three-fourths of the total expenditure is borne by the States. The HEIs are highly dependent on Government support and financial crises like budgetary deficits and rise in prices adversely affect the financial health of universities and colleges, which, in turn, prove to be determental to the promotion of higher quality of relevant programmes.

For an intensive study of different facets of university systems' performance a purposive selection of fifteen (15) universities has been made, out of the oldest institutions established before 1968. These universities represent different regions, types of institutions like Central and States universities as well as unitary, affiliating and residential types, etc. These together enrol 20 per cent of the total enrolment in higher education in the country. The following features are noteworthy.

The sample as a whole enroles 68 per cent of the total students in social sciences, arts and humanities while the remaining students pursue scientific and technical disciplines. These percentages for the sample universities are comparable with the overall respective ratios for the higher education in the country.

The financial dependence of these universities on the government widely differs, in the range of 7.5 to 97.4 per cent of the total income, though for most universities grant-in-aid-received from the government is the single major source of income. The examination fees, particularly in the affiliating universities constitutes a major source of income (16 to 30 per cent). Likewise, collection of fees from distance learners in the dual mode universities is an important source of income. The contributions of tuition fee alone is about 5 to 10 per cent in most universities. An assessment of university finances reveal that: (a) the Central universities are more dependent (90 per cent and above) on the government than the State universities, some of which receive less than 50 per cent of the total income as grants; (b) the universities differ in their relative efforts to mobilise resources from alternative sources; and (c) there is a great scope to benefit from each other's experience in resource mobilisation from different alternative sources.

As may be expected, the pattern of utilisation of funds differ due mainly to the differences in areas and extent of specialisation in higher education activities. The share of expenditure on non-academic activities is generally very high (50 to 60 per cent) in most universities. Faculty and discipline-wise analyses of the pattern in allocation of resources for various purposes, with respect to each university provide useful in sights into the aspects of prudence in use of funds.

Cost-Efficiency

The extent to which various programmes offered by the universities are cost efficient is examined on the basis of unit costs (per student) of relevant services. The results indicate the degree of variations in allocation of financial resources at the aggregative as well as disaggregative levels. The relevant comparisons, based on alternative estimates of unit costs on the basis of weighted (and absolute) enrolment to minimise distortions due to factors like nature, type and levels of programmes, indicate the magnitude of over or under funding of programmes in relation to the average level of expenditure by the select universities. The methodology of estimation of the unit costs may be useful to determine the amount which may be recovered from the beneficiaries under various heads of expenditure-teaching and non-teaching support services–in order that funding of HEIs is rationalised on equity and efficiency grounds.

The results show that the annual average per student cost of higher education in the country, in 1988-89, was eighteen thousand in universities, thirty-one thousand in 'deemed' universities and seventy-two thousand in the institutions of national importance. About 32 per cent and 20-24 per cent of the total costs was accounted for by the payment of salaries of teaching and non-teaching staff, respectively. On the basis of the select universities, the average discipline-wise per unit costs indicate wide differences ranging from as low as thirteen thousand for Political Science to as high as forty-five thousand for Anthropology. Likewise, for the science disciplines the unit costs varies between thirty-three thousand for Statistics to sixty thousand for Chemistry. The unit costs of Engineering and Medical sciences comes to Rs. 1.3 and 1.5 lakhs per year respectively. More than 50 per cent of these costs are accounted for by the central administration and common services. Clearly, even for the comparable programmes having theoretical parity, the results clearly demonstrate considerable differences in financial inputs (unit costs) as measured by coefficient of variations (CVs). The major reasons that are attributable to variations in unit costs are: lack of application of objective criteria for determination of requirements of funds by the funding agencies, differences in structure of the scale of pay of non-teaching staff which consume almost 50 per cent of the total salary payments, differences in the degree of specialisation in professional and technical disciplines vis-a-vis general courses in higher education, the nature and type of university-unitary, affiliating, residential, etc., which significantly influence the central (administrative) costs, mainly administration, maintenance of building, etc. It is difficult to indicate the extent to which each of the above factor is responsible for causing variations in unit costs. However, the detailed decomposition of costs separately for each institution, as attempted in this study, allow for obtaining an idea about the factors which influence the cost structure at the desirable disaggregation level. In brief, there is much to be desired insofar as internal-efficiency, as judged on comparative basis from various uses of funds in terms of unit costs, is concerned.

Cost-Effectiveness

Against the backdrop of allocation of resources for various types of programmes i.e. input costs per student, the students' performance as measured by examination results are assessed to obtain an idea about the cost-effectiveness of academic disciplines, which obviously give an indication of the quality of educated manpower produced by the system to manage multifarious socio-economic activities of the society. The results, however, belie the *a priori* positive expectation about the relationship between magnitude of input costs and levels of learning attainments. Specifically, the results demonstrate (i) considerable wastage of resources as about 60 per cent of student pass and merely 13 per cent of those who pass score more than 60 per cent marks, (ii) a lower degree of emphasis for promotion of technical and professional education, which holds the key to modernisation of economy and (iii) a lower level of achievements with respect to 'academic excellence'.

To gain an idea about the cost effectiveness of various programmes, the level of students' attainments is examined in relation to the input costs, which reveal the following. First, there is urgent need to probe into the causes and effects of low productivity of the university system as the evidence on the magnitude of costs and performance is quite mixed. Second, the quality of education, particularly in humanities and social sciences is very poor as a significant majority of students pass with low score of marks. This is true even when the unit costs are higher in some institutions. It emerges therefore, that the reasons for lack of cost effectiveness of university programmes should not be traced in the costs and finance aspects of higher education alone, which though important, are influenced by the factors like effective planning and management of programmes for improving performance with respect to given level of allocation of resources. In effect, HEIs suffer from both internal as well as external efficiency, and therefore, all the stakeholders i.e. students, parents, teachers and the planners should pay urgent attention to vitalize the functioning of institutions by initiating corrective measures.

Major Policy Inferences

Of the major recommendations that emerge from the findings of this study, the following are noteworthy. First, an equitable approach of funding based on objective assessment of needs requires to be evolved by the funding agencies, particularly with respect to comparable programmes offered by various institutions. The policy and pattern of funding should be consistent with the policy of maintaining theoretical parity and uniform standard of courses offered by various institutions in the Indian federation. In determining the eligibility for block grants for each university, academic performance, efficiency in use of funds and manpower needs should *inter alia* be given due consideration. Second, the mechanism of resource allocation should be used as an instrument of raising internal and external efficiency of various programmes of higher education, training and research. It would require, *inter alia*, establishing effective linkages between the aspects of funding education and development activities that are dependent on educational inputs. In fact, quality of relevant programmes and other socio-economic factors should receive due weightage in influencing the resource allocation policy. Third, the opportunities for learning by relaxing the constraints on expansion and diversification of higher education programmes, should be augmented. This would require a greater degree of transparency in the arrangements for financing the programmes from different sources and/or sharing the burden of costs of education among different beneficiary groups. A conducive policy environment should be created to make the beneficiaries pay, as they benefit from education, out of current or future incomes to ensure financial sustenance of the system. The measures for financial reforms should focus on improving academic and financial accountability of the system through a better understanding between the providers and beneficiaries of university services. Finally, in the wake of increasing globalisation of economy, responsiveness of the higher education system to the changes in economy and the society should be improved mainly by establishing effective linkages between institutions and development sectors to enable the system to produce requisite number and calibre of manpower needed for raising productivity and competitiveness of economy.

ONE

INTRODUCTION

The Approach and Framework of Analysis

> Higher Education provides people with an opportunity to reflect on the critical social, economic, cultural, moral and spiritual issues facing humanity. It contributes to national development through dissemination of specialized knowledge and skills. It is therefore a crucial factor for survival.
>
> — *National Policy on Education 1986* (para 5.24)

Preamble

The perceived socio-economic value of higher education, especially to transform the Indian society into a more enlightened, prosperous and civilized community has been duly recognised ever since the inception of planning era, in 1951. The educational policies have therefore accorded high priority for development of high quality of relevant education and training to meet the manpower requirements of every development sector.[1] To realise this objective, a number of policy decisions have been taken from time to time which have led to considerable expansion and diversification of university system; and accordingly, growth in government expenditure on higher education has also been manifold. Yet, the increasing financial needs of the universities to cope with the challenges that confront them, especially in providing high quality of relevant courses and in carrying out academic programmes in frontier areas of knowledge and innovation of technology remain unmet.

Inadequacy of financial inputs and lack of effective management of resources are mainly responsible for less than expected level of performance of universities.[2] Empirical evidence[3] has, for instance, revealed that while a number of universities (45) (60 per cent) suffered from perpetual budgetary deficits during the block of five years 1984-

89, a significant number (35) (40 per cent) of universities enjoyed surpluses. An emerging view therefore is that cost-effectiveness of university education suffers from mis-allocation of resources or lack of effective management of academic programmes, while inadequacy of funds contribute to uneconomic use of resources.. As the programmes of higher education are not duly responsive to manpower needs of modern economy, as evident from mis-match between education and job requirements, an important question that emanate is: how to vitalize university system? Of late, there is therefore, increased policy emphasis on devising ways and means of improving performance and accountability of colleges and universities to ensure the supply of competent manpower to manage the society and economy.[4]

Since the universities are mainly financed by the Government, the Centre and the States, a number of pertinent questions have been raised on the grounds of both equity and efficiency, in the literature on economic aspects of higher education.[5] While a considerable amount of time and effort have been devoted to examine the sources and methods of financing higher education, the empirical exercises on the manner in which resources are utilized by the universities or the pattern of allocation funds within the institutions for meeting the requirements of academic and non-academic programmes, are very limited. No idea is, therefore, gained to indicate the areas and extent of diseconomies in carrying out the programmes of teaching and research. This is, however, no surprising because the funding agencies namely the Departments of Education of the Central and the State Governments as well as the University Grants Commission (UGC) do not determine eligibility of an institution for block grants on the basis of financial and academic accountability, howsoever measured for the purpose.[6] Also, they do not even stipulate, for the recipient universities, to ensure effective utilization of resources as judged by the accepted performance indicators. With a view to ensuring sound planning and efficient management of financial resources, the development and use of efficiency norms are, therefore, indispensable. In this context, estimation of unit costs of education and identification of its various components which account for the major share of costs are of paramount importance for assessing the performance of an institutions vis-a-vis other institutions, on comparative basis, with a view to obtaining an idea of cost-effectiveness of varying programmes. Educational planners and decision-makers are always interested in gauging the performance of institutions to justify investments in them and their programmes as well as to design appropriate policy interventions. Hence, this exercise.

1.2 Rationale of the Study

Universities consume a significant amount of nation's resources, about 15 per cent of the total educational outlays. Mis-utilization of resources in the university sector constitutes a real welfare loss as much as the economic benefits foregone in any commercial sector due to misallocation of funds. Also, as the quality and relevance of university outputs in the form of educated and trained graduates and research activities have significant bearing on productivity of other socio-economic sectors, the production of goods and services suffers due to inefficiency in the management of universities. The prevailing financial exigency and on-going economic reforms have necessitated a closer scrutiny of various socio-economic programmes funded by the Government with a view to rationalising the subsidization policy with respect to various economic services. It is, therefore, invetible to undertake a detailed investigation into the causes of what ails the financial health of universities and also to explore ways and measures to make effective use of limited funds.

The diagnostic studies[7] pertaining to the degree of efficiency in use of funds and the prescriptions of financial norms derived therefrom for financing educational programmes are generally based on costs analyses which have proved to be a powerful tool for sound planning and effective management of financial resources. The analysis of unit costs mainly in terms of per student indicate the areas and extent of changes that are required to be effected, keeping especially in view the changes in other inter-related parameters relating to the promotion of education and its linkages with other socio-economic sectors. Cost analysis is thus used by the educational planners to improve internal as well as external efficiency of programmes by introducing suitable changes in the structure of input costs of different programmes and institutions. It may be emphasised that cost analysis is useful when the unit costs are compared with other alternative mode of delivery of services and that in relation to some measure of outcome, mainly in terms of learning attainments.

Inspite of the fact that the uses of costs analysis for innovation and efficient management of university system are well known, there has been no worthwhile attempt to estimate the costs of higher education programmes offered by a cross-section of universities under the aegis of the Central and the State Governments. In absence of such informative and useful data as per student costs, it is not known as to why and to what extent input costs vary, particularly when there is well recognised parity of degrees awarded by the various universities? What are the sources of variations in the input costs of higher education and to what extent different factors account for them? Is there any relationship between a high or low input costs vis-a-vis the students' performance as assessed by some measure of students' learning achievements? Is there sound justification for evolving scientific norms of allocating resources for various university programmes and, if so, is it possible to do so on the basis of existing data and the current funding mechanisms as adopted by the concerned agencies of the Centre and the State?

In brief, is there the need to evolve an effective funding mechanism to seek the value for money invested in higher education as well as to make the university system responsive to the challenge of development that confront the nation today?

No claim is made in this study to fully answer all of these question, but an attempt is made to focus on different dimensions of costs and effectiveness of university programmes; which, given the usual limitations of an investigator, the data and tools of analysis, deals primarily with all the relevant questions raised above.

1.3 The Focus and Scope of Study

An attempt has been made in this study to analyse cross-sectional financial data (actual) for the year 1988-89 mainly in terms of relevant ratios and percentages as well as per student costs at both institutional level and disaggregated levels i.e. at the faculty and departmental levels. The relevant comparisons of sources of finance, patterns of allocation of funds across the teaching departments and unit costs (per student) among a group of fifteen (15) universities of different types and from different regions have been made. The criteria of selection of universities are indicated below. Only those having comparable programmes have been examined to indicate the relative level of costs and the factors that accounted for them. The study attempts to make a comparative analysis of patterns of allocation of funds for various uses, indicates the extent of variations in different physical and financial indicators and compares the differences in costs with the learning attainments so as to gain some idea about the cost-effectiveness of educational programmes in the select universities. It is hoped that such comparisons would lend desirable perspective on resource allocation for higher education with a view to improving efficiency of universities.

Though the degree of educational efforts and levels of attainments vary, the policy for human resource development through education has been desirably uniform among the federating States as per the provisions of the Constitution of India. The resources for providing financial sustenance of the universities largely come from the central pool of resources, irrespectives of the channel through which money flow to them. Why is then the approach of funding comparable programmes that have theoretical parity throughout the country is not uniform? Without ensuring equity in provisions of Government supported programmes other things being equal is it possible to contain and maintain inter-personal differences in educational attainments across the institutions and regions? The answer would probably be in negative. In fact, this is one of the major motivating factor behind the endeavours to present the results of various exercises undertaken on comparative basis in this study, which reveals the extent of divergence in allocation and utilization of funds as well as academic performance.

The scope of the present study is limited and confined to merely fifteen (15) universities, of which ten (10) belongs to the category of teaching and affiliated and the remaining five (5) are teaching and residential. In the former category are included the universities of Bombay (Maharashtra), Calcutta (West Bengal), Gauhati (Assam), H.S. Gaur (Madhya Pradesh), Kerala (Kerala), Kurukshetra (Haryana), Madras (Tamil Nadu), Mysore (Karnataka), Panjab (Punjab), and Utkal (Orissa). All of these universities are obviously from different States of the Indian federation, offer programmes in different disciplines at undergraduate and post-graduate levels and all of them are State universities. In the other category are the Universities of Annamalai (Tamil Nadu), Banaras (Uttar Pradesh), Delhi and Jawaharlal Nehru (Delhi) and Visva Bharati (West Bengal). All these universities, except Annamalai, are Central and have established their own marks in the promotion of higher education in the country. As all of them were established before 1970, it may be said that they have overtime streamlined their functioning in tune with the given objectives of promoting higher education and research.

A detailed profile of the fifteen universities in the sample are presented in Chapter 2. It is important to mention that while an attempt was made to select a large number of universities of various types from different States, the choice got restricted due to non-availability of data for cost analysis as we heavily depended on the supply of relevant documents from the universities. The analysis is, moreover, confined to university teaching departments and constituent colleges while the affiliated colleges are out of the purview of this study. Admittedly, the study of college finances and cost-effectiveness of their programme is important to develop perspectives about this segment of university system which makes a major contribution to higher education in the country, particularly by way of performing teaching functions with respect to about 85 per cent of the total enrolment in universities and colleges. But, their activities are restricted mainly to teaching and more so in the area of general higher education, mostly at undergraduate levels (87 per cent). Therefore, due to time and resource constraints, the study is confined to university teaching departments which have significant bearing on the overall education system. The results are worked out and presented in such a way as to allow for drawing relevant inferences to generalise the conclusions, with, of course, usual limitations that emanate from conceptual and statistical problems. Professional institutions like Agricultural universities, Medical and Technical institutions, namely IITs are also not covered in the study, though the professional education imparted by the Central and the State universities, covered in the study, have been duly examined to reflect the unit costs of such education. Like-wise self financing institutions of higher learning, some of which are under the category of 'deemed to be university', are also not examined in this study.

1.4 The Data and Approach of Analysis

As the study seeks to analyse per student institutional costs of higher education, the relevant financial data, as described below, have been suitably re-arranged to ensure comparability. This was necessitated because the universities do not have uniform format of presentation of physical and financial data. Also, such data were obtained from two different sources of records of the respective universities. For instance, the data on students' enrolment, teachers and other non-teaching staff are obtained from the Annual Reports of universities which do not provide the necessary break up of data to allow for making disaggragative analysis. Likewise, the financial data obtained from the university budgets/Annual Accounts are not shown separately for undergraduate and postgraduate education and research under the stream of general and professional/technical higher education. In some universities, the items of recurring and non-recurring expenditure differ a great deal which indicate that not only the concepts of financial terms in vogue differ across the universities but also the procedure of maintenance of data varies. Without going into much details of budgetary systems of Indian universities, the entire financial data were re-classified on the basis of broad patterns as followed by most universities; and accordingly, data were clubbed under recurring and non-recurring expenditure, the relevant components of which are indicated below:

Recurring expenditure refers to the expenditure under both plan and non-plan which are incurred every year on continuing basis for carrying out on going programmes of teaching and research. While there are inter-university difference in plan and non-plan expenditure, the latter broadly constitutes more than three-fourths of the total expenditure. The magnitude of recurrding expenditure under this category varies directly in proportion to the size of salary bill for teaching and non-teaching staff and the financial requirements for other consumable items. The amount of expenditure under these categories is determined by the past trend or committed liability under the plan and non-plan, rather than the number of students in different types and levels of programmes and the nature and level of research activities. The requirements on account of changes in the prices are duly provided for by the Government. The major heads of recurring expenditure are: Salaries of teaching and non-teaching staff, maintenance of common services like repair of buildings, roads, maintenance of gardens, health centres, water and electricity supply, provisions for students' services namely sports and games and other cultural activities, maintenance of libraries and expenses on conduct of examinations, etc.

In the category of non-recurring expenditure are included construction of building, purchase of furniture, equipment, books and journals, etc. The expenditure in this category accounts for about 10 per cent of the total expenditure. Since all the universities covered in this study are well established much before 1970, the analysis of recurring expenditure alone can lend perspectives on efficiency in use of resources. It may be reiterated that the components of recurring and non-recurring expenditure, as indicated above, have been suitably classified to reflect the educational activities on the lines of teaching functions, central administration and other student support services to represent the total institutional costs.

The results of various exercises based on recurring expenditure have been presented in the categories of payment of salaries to teaching and non-teaching staff and other expenses on non-salary items; and, thus, the relevant results are presented at the Institutional, Faculty and Departmental levels. Care has been taken to show results separately for academic, administrative and common services. In doing so, two sets of data have been generated. While one pertains to academic services in which case faculty-wise and department-wise data have been analysed, the other set of results relate to Central expenses which show the break up of expenditure on administration, common services, student services, library and examination, mainly under the salary and non-salary items of expenditure incurred by the offices of Vice-Chancellor, Pro-Vice-Chancellor, Registrar, Finance, Estate office etc. The relevant details and the components of expenditure under each of the above head are presented and discussed in Chapter 3. The total central costs have been distributed along the faculty and departmental costs on *pro-rata* basis.

Furthermore, two sets of per student expenditure have been estimated; one relates to unweighted (absolute) unit costs which have been worked out by dividing the total expenditure by the absolute total enrolment while another pertain to weighted (per student equivalent) unit costs which have been obtained by dividing total expenditure by the suitably weighted enrolment which reflect relative magnitude of costs due to the nature, quality and level of education. The details of the method of computation and the rationale for assigning differential weights for arriving at equivalent student enrolment for various programmes of studies are described in Chapter 3, where the relevant results are discussed. The estimates of weighted unit costs would hopefully make the results comparable which is otherwise not possible due to the diversities of characteristics of universities and the different nature and types of programmes offered by them.

Wherever possible, an endeavour has been made to make use of reliable indicators to explain the financial situation obtaining in all or the concerned universities. As may be expected in a comparative study, such as this, care has been taken to compile data on comparable basis and desirable consistency has also been maintained in the analysis and presentation of data throughout the study. In interpreting results, however, abundant care should be exercised because the social settings, the system and structure of university system in India are extremely diverse as discussed in Chapter 2; and the system is therefore not always amenable to objective economic analysis. Also, the nature and quality of relevant data do not allow for employing rigorous statistical techniques for drawing appropriate and unambigous conclusions. For instance, as may be observed later in this study, inter-university difference in availability of physical and financial resources are so wide that the approach of econometric analysis cannot be employed for a small number of fifteen universities. In fact, we have made an attempt to carry out econometric exercises but the emerging results, as judged from the goodness of the fit, are not tenable. They are, therefore, not presented and discussed in this study.

A word about the limitation of data and approach of analysis may be mentioned. First, as the data on expenditure are not maintained by the universities for various programmes separately, the data were therefore reclassified and clubbed suitably to reflect the pattern of expenditure by major activities. On a number of occasions difficulties arose about the inclusion or exclusion of certain items. Due to error of judgement, the data could marginally distort the relative level of unit costs, especially those worked out on the basis of absolute or unweighted enrolment. Whenever such adjustment has been made, it has been mentioned at the appropriate place.

Second, the differential weights assigned to various levels and programmes of education on the basis of the concept of 'value added' to educational attainments at the successive levels of graduation cannot be scientifically proved as appropriate factor for showing the normative or positive differences in costs. Yet, because of the theoretical reasons for cost differences due to the level and nature of programmes, the relevant weights have been evolved and adopted on the basis of our judgement of prevailing financial management of universities so as to reflect the variations in costs of education. This could be hazardous exercise but there was no option owing to missing data links and the strong theoretical underpining for demostrating unit costs of various programmes of higher education on comparable basis.

Third, keeping in view the vastness of the Indian higher education system, a mere study of fifteen universities is not enough to generalise results for the entire system; more so because, the glaring differences among them in respects of all the considered variables did not allow for employing rigorous statistical methods like regression analysis. These limitations of the data and approach of analysis should be borne in mind throughout the discussions on unit costs. Finally, without dwelling deep into the financial or economic concepts of cost and expenditure, these terms have been used in this study inter changeably.

1.5 Scheme of Presentation of the Study

The development of higher education in India and its financing are discussed in Chapter 2, which provides a brief background of the aspects of expansion and diversification of the university activities both at the national as well as regional levels. The attention is focused on the sources and methods of financing different types of higher education institutions. Against this backdrop, the sources of revenue and patterns of expenditure of the fifteen (15) universities covered in this study are presented so as to place the analysis of costs and its financing in proper context of the study. The individual profile of universities presented, though briefly, in this chapter should prove to be useful for drawing relevant inferences for planning and management of resources in a university as compared to the situations obtaining in other universities.

The results of unit costs analysis are presented in Chapter 3, which demonstrate the costs of higher education at the institutional, faculty and departmental levels. The break of expenditure by major categories like salaries and non-salaries are provided to reflect the composition and patterns of internal allocation of funds under the major heads and sub-heads of academic and central expenses. The sources and extent of variations in unit costs are also discussed.

The aspects of efficiency in performance are discussed in Chapter 4, which focuses on comparative assessment of efficiency as assessed in terms of students' learning attainments. The use of indicators like unit costs, examination results, student-teacher ratios, etc., assist in gaining an idea of internal efficiency in management of universities. In essence, cost-effectiveness analysis is attempted in this Chapter.

The last Chapter 5, discusses policy implications for university development, emanating mainly from the findings of the study and other related issues. This chapter hints at policy options with regard to mechanism of funding, improvement in cost-efficiency and mobilization of resources such that cost-effectiveness of university programmes could be desirably improved and made responsive to the challenges of development.

NOTES AND REFERENCES

1. See the Reports of *University Education Commission, 1948 and Education Commission (1964-66)* Government of India, which have duly emphasised the need for vitalizing higher education system to cope with the challenge of development.
2. See, Ch. 7 of author's *Fiscal Policy for University Development*, Concept.
3. *Financial Deficits in Universities*, AIU, 1992.
4. For a detailed discussion on different aspects of higher education development see, *Higher Education in India: Retrospect and Prospect*, (ed.) by Moonis Raza, AIU, 1991.
5. National Policy on Education: Programme of Action, 1986 and Author's *Fiscal Policy for University Development*, Concept.
6. See author's *Fiscal Policy. op. cit.*
7. *Ibid.*, and *UGC Funding of Institutions of Higher Education* (1993) Report of Justice Dr. K. Punnayya Committee.

TWO

DEVELOPMENT OF HIGHER EDUCATION

Growth of Institutions, Enrolment and Finance

In the fast changing socio-economic context, the higher education system has continued to be exposed to greater pressures for expansion and diversification mainly because of the demands for social justice in the provision of educational services, for providing a training ground for educated, manpower to meet the needs of the expanding industry, trade and commerce, for initiating and manging social change or just for intellectual curiosity. It also seems difficult to restrict the entry of unmotivated students in higher education system, who in absence of worthwhile alternative avenues of education and employment stay in the system. The availability of adequate funds to cope with the growing requirements of higher education is likely to be much more difficult due to the factors like general paucity of funds and competing claims of different priority areas like removal of poverty and eradication of illiteracy. Lack of application of low cost technologies and inability of the conventional university system to generate sufficient degree of economies of scale have made the higher education programmes cost prohibitive.

In the prevailing situation which lays emphasis on promotion of elementary and vocational education, the funding of higher education would therefore require greater scrutiny as it is considered that 'there is no justification for heavy subsidization of higher education by the Government to the extent being done today,[1] especially because the beneficiaries of higher education are generally better the off section of society and that the private benefits are higher than social gains. In the Eighth Five Year Plan, policy emphasis is clearly laid on the development of education but the general higher education has the least priority as evident from the declining share of plan allocation. The allocation of plan outlays of Rs. 700 crores in the Eighth Plan (1992-97) for higher education as against Rs. 541 in the Seventh Plan (1985-90) is inadequate to offset the erosion of real value of money due to considerable rise in prices, recent devaluation of money and the committed liability of establishing new Central universities. The level of allocation for higher education is likely to be even lower or inadequate to meet the financial requirements for the committed programmes due to perpetuation of financial exigency and the national urgency to fulfil Constitutional commitment of creating necessary provisions for elementary education and removal of adult illiteracy. It has been duly noted in the context of Central Government's Budget for 1996-97 that "The central allocation has declined from Rs. 246 crore to Rs. 238 crore. Since the central plan grants are provided on matching basis to the state universities, there would obviously be reduced level of funding by the states also, whose fiscal capacity is no better than the Centre. Higher education is therefore bound to suffer even more than in the past as the requirements for upgradation of programmes is high and rising, and the sources of funds drying."[2] The universities and colleges are therefore passing through a period of financial stringency since the resources available to them are much less than sufficient to cope with increased needs for improving the responsiveness of the higher education programmes to the changing needs of the society and economy. The emerging developments, in the contexts of both higher education as well as the general economic scene of the country, indicate that higher educational institutions have to compete for limited funds for their own sustenance and for realizing their objectives of ensuring human resources development through education.[3]

In view of the foregoing, an attempt is made below to discern the trend of growth of institutions, enrolments and finance with a view to evolving perspectives for future;[4] and against the backdrop of overall changing scenario of higher education in India, a brief profile of the 15 universities, which are chosen for this study, would be placed in the context. In doing so, a detailed background about the nature and type of universities, distribution of teaching and non-teaching staff, students enrolment by level, sources of income and pattern of allocation of expenditure will be discussed. Hopefully, such a background material would be conducive for appraising the relevant results presented and discussed in the subsequent Chapters.

2.1 Nature and Type of Universities

In accordance with the provisions of the Constitution of India, the responsibility of ensuring development of education is entrusted to both the levels of Governments, the Centre and the States. They are therefore empowered to establish and/or sponsor institutions for promotion of all types and levels of education. The major responsibility of promoting education has generally develoved on the States for historical reasons and this holds true for higher education also as a significant majority of universities and colleges have been established and are funded by the States. Due to the diversities of geographic regions and socio-economic settings, different types of institutions have come up mainly in response to the demands for satisfying manpower needs of the economy as well as individual intellectual curiosity.

A number of universities, which have been established by the Centre and the States, to accommodate social demand for higher education belong to the affiliating and teaching type in which university departments impart instruction mainly at the postgraduate level and undertake research. These universities have a large number of colleges affiliated to them to cater for undergraduate education. Some colleges also have postgraduate teaching and research. There are also a few unitary type universities which do not have affiliated colleges but they do have university departments/constituent colleges. In most of them, there is undergraduate and postgraduate teaching as well as research. There are also some universities which are in some sense a mixture of the two types. Their territorial jurisdiction is usually confined to the city in which the university is located. The colleges located within the city are affiliated to the university. Some of the colleges are, however, managed by the university and are known as its constituent colleges, Delhi University is a typical example of this type The unitary and affiliating universities have been established under both the sectors—the Centre and the States. Most of the universities of these types have residential facilities to provide campus based teaching and research programmes for a large number of students. Such universities are therefore also known as teaching and residential universities. Table 2.1, provides an idea of the teaching, affiliating and residential

TABLE 2.1: Nature and Type of Select Universities

S. No.	Universities	Year of establishment	Jurisdiction of the University	Type of University	No. of Affiliated and constituent colleges
1	2	3	4	5	6
1.	Annamalai (SU)	1929	Radius of ten miles from the Univ. Convocation Hall at Annamalainagar	Unitary and Residential	—
2.	BHU (CU)	1916	Within a radius of 15 miles from the main Temple	Teaching and Residential	4 affiliated, 1 Constituent College and 23 Institutions
3.	Bombay (SU)	1957	Greater Bombay, Konkan Distt. Ratangiri and Goa	Teaching, Affiliating and Federal	205 Constituent/ Affiliated Colleges
4.	Calcutta (SU)	1857	State of West Bengal and Tripura	Teaching and Affiliating	206 Affiliated and 4 Univ. Collges
5.	Delhi (CU)	1922	Whole of Delhi	Teaching and Affiliating	1 Constituent 64 Affiliated colleges
6.	Gauhati (SU)	1948	Assam (Exld. Distts. of Lakhimpur, Dibrugarh and Sibsagar	Teaching, Residential and Affiliating	117 Affiliated colleges
7.	HS Gaur (SU)	1946	Revenue Distt. of Balghat, Betul, Chhindwara, Damoh, Nimas, Hoshangabad, Sagar	Teaching, Residential and Affiliating	93 Affiliated colleges

(Contd.)

TABLE 2.1 *(Contd.)*

1	2	3	4	5	6
8.	JNU (CU)	1968	The whole of India	Residential and Unitary	Univ. has 8 recognized institutions
9.	Kerala (SU)	1937	Revenue Dist. of Trivandrum Quilon, Alleppey, Kottayam, Iddikki and Ernakulam	Teaching Residential and Affiliating	60 Affiliated colleges
10.	Kurukshetra (SU)	1956	Dist. Ambala, Hissar, Jind, Karnal, Kurukshetra and Sirsa	Teaching and Affiliating	70 Affiliated 2 Univ. Colleges
11.	Madras (SU)	1857	Madras State (excluding Madurai Ramanathapuram, Kanya Kumari) and U.T. Pondicherry	Teaching and Affiliating	104 Affiliated and 7 institutions
12.	Mysore (SU)	1916	Dist. of Mysore, Mandya, Hassan, Chickmagulur, Shimoga and Chitradurga	Affiliating	116 Affiliated 6 Univ. Colleges
13.	Panjab (SU)	1947	The jurisdiction of this Univ. has not been technically defined	Affiliating and Teaching	93 Affiliated 1 institute
14.	Utkal (SU)	1943	Dist. of Cuttak, Puri, Balasore, Mayur Bhanj, Keonjhare, Dhenkanal	Affiliating	206 Affiliated Colleges and 2 constituent
15.	Visva Bharati (CU)	1951	The area of Shantiniketan (11.5 sq. miles) in the Dist. of Birbhum	Unitary, Teaching and Residential	7 Constituent Colleges

Note: CU - Central University; SU - State University

Source: University Development in India, 1977-78 to 1986-87, Pt. I, Section A, UGC, New Delhi.

universities in India, which are the subject matter of this study.

There are those universities which are largely, if not exclusively, affiliating in nature. They do not have campus teaching but their main responsibility, *inter alia*, is to conduct examinations with respect to affiliating colleges. The major universities in this category are: Agra, Meerut, Jiwaji, Awadh, etc. There are also those institutions which are known as 'deemed to be' universities which are recognised under the article 17 of the UGC. The universities/institutes in this category are primarily unitary type to cater to the specific needs in almost every branch of education. The aspects of administration and financial governance of institutions in this category greatly varies to which we shall return later.

The professional universities established with stress on research and extension work in the fields of agriculture and technical education constitute another type. The number of such universities is quite large as pointed out below. In addition to these, there are now six Institutes of Technology and almost an equal number of medical institutes which have been set up by an act of Parliament as Institutes of National Importance and form another category.

2.2 Growth in the Number of Institutions and Enrolments

Higher education in India has recorded a phenomenal growth and has emerged out to be the second largest, after the USA, in the world. The number of universities has risen from 28 in 1950-51 to 220 (as per AIU list) by the end of 1996 registering a more than seven fold increase. Table 2.2 presents a comprehensive picture about the distribution of institutions for various levels and types of education, for 1990-91, across the States. It shows wide differences in the states effort to establish institutions for providing education and training to eligible group to students.

In addition, the number of affiliated colleges has also increased by nearly ten times, from 695 in 1950-51 to 6597 in 1987-88 (Table 2.3). The total number of colleges has however reached to 7121 in 1990-91. The newly established colleges provide an idea of the nature of expansion and diversification of education. Of the 85 such new colleges in 1987-88 (Table 2.3), 74 were arts/science/commerce colleges while the remaining were mainly professional colleges belonging to different faculties of Technology, Law and Agriculture. Obviously, the expansion is more towards the general higher

TABLE 2.2: Educational Institutions by Levels, 1990-1

S. No.	State/Union	Primary	Middle	High School/Colleges for			
				Hr. Sec./ Intermediate Pre-degree/ Jr. Colleges	General Education	Professional Education	Univer-sities*
1	2	3	4	5	6	7	8
1.	Andhra Pradesh	48731	6118	6695	403	82	17
2.	Arunachal Pradesh	1122	254	113	4	0	1
3.	Assam	28876	5703	3443	213	15	3
4.	Bihar	53252	13170	4097	557	31	11
5.	Goa	1014	112	372	15	4	1
6.	Gujarat	13174	17084	5075	230	59	10
7.	Haryana	4922	1321	2266	119	22	4
8.	Himachal Pradesh	7522	1101	1037	39	4	3
9.	Jammu & Kashmir	8712	2320	1097	27	9	3
10.	Karnataka	23539	16318	5110	403	132	9
11.	Kerala	6772	2911	2568	133	31	6
12.	Madhya Pradesh	66849	13977	3973	448	37	12
13.	Maharashtra	39121	18849	10374	582	195	18

(Contd.)

TABLE 2.2 (Contd.)

1	2	3	4	5	6	7	8
14.	Manipur	3226	693	440	31	4	1
15.	Meghalaya	4163	693	303	23	1	1
16.	Mizoram	1109	544	205	13	1	1
17.	Nagaland	1287	341	148	15	1	0
18.	Orissa	40033	9405	4926	244	20	5
19.	Punjab	12372	1425	2743	171	26	4
20.	Rajasthan	30231	8629	3733	159	41	9
21.	Sikkim	510	122	75	1	0	0
22.	Tamil Nadu	29979	5624	5158	214	71	15
23.	Tripura	2083	436	454	13	2	1
24.	Uttar Pradesh	76545	14582	5999	418	24	25
25.	West Bengal	50827	4179	6804	302	62	11
26.	A&N Islands	186	41	66	2	1	0
27.	Chandigarh	54	27	68	12	2	2
28.	Dadra & Nagar Haveli	120	41	11	0	0	0
29.	Daman & Diu	46	20	19	1	0	0
30.	Delhi	1655	485	1130	63	6	11

(Contd.)

TABLE 2.2 *(Contd.)*

1	2	3	4	5	6	7	8
31.	Lakshadweep	19	4	11	0	0	0
32.	Pondicherry	341	107	106	7	3	1
	India	558392	146636	78619	4862	886	184

* Includes Deemed Universities and Institutions of National Importance.

Source: Selected Educational Statistics, 1990-91, Ministry of Human Resource Development, Govt. of India, New Delhi.

TABLE 2.3: Growth and Expansion of Colleges by Major Areas of Study (1983-84 to 1987-88)

S. No.	Courses of Study	Number of Colleges					% increase during the period 1983-84 to 1987-88
		1983-84	1984-85	1985-86	1986-87	1987-88	
1	2	3	4	5	6	7	8
1.	Arts/Science/ Commerce	3758	4004	4132	4354	4428	17.8
2.	Technical/ Professional	563	618	655	695	719	27.7
3.	Law	186	194	199	202	204	9.7
4.	Physical Education/ Education	391	430	441	479	470	20.2
5.	Oriental Learning	283	277	321	720	714	152.3
6.	Music/Fine Arts	65	67	68	62	62	4.6
	Total	5246	5590	5816	6512	6597	25.7

1. Junior colleges and colleges offering only diploma courses are not taken into account.

Source: Annual Report for the year 1988-89, University Grants Commission, New Delhi.

TABLE 2.4: Growth in Number of Colleges by the States (1983-84 to 1987-88)

S. No.	States/Union	Number of Colleges (UC + AC)					Increase during the period 1983-84 to 1987-88	
		1983-84	1984-85	1985-86	1986-87	1987-88		
1	2	3	4	5	6	7	8	%age
1.	Andhra Pradesh	420	470	492	495	494	74	(17.6)
2.	Arunachal Pradesh	—	—	—	3	3	3	(0.0)
3.	Assam	154	162	171	180	180	26	(16.9)
4.	Bihar	472	509	568	617	632	159	(33.6)
5.	Goa	—	—	—	19	19	19	(0.0)
6.	Gujarat	285	295	302	311	317	32	(11.2)
7.	Haryana	143	143	143	142	147	32	(22.4)
8.	Himachal Pradesh	27	27	33	34	40	13	(48.1)
9.	Jammu & Kashmir	41	89	39	41	41	0	(0.0)
10.	Karnataka	128	535	556	603	644	516	(403.1)
11.	Kerala	184	184	188	200	200	16	(8.7)
12.	Madhya Pradesh	396	445	472	502	570	174	(43.9)
13.	Maharashtra	693	801	834	874	865	172	(24.8)
14.	Manipur	22	23	23	23	23	1	(4.5)

(Contd.)

TABLE 2.4 *(Contd.)*

1	2	3	4	5	6	7	8	%age
15.	Meghalaya/Nagaland	33	34	34	37	38	5	(15.5)
16.	Orissa	179	215	225	240	252	73	(15.5)
17.	Punjab	228	228	226	231	230	2	(40.8)
18.	Rajasthan	221	222	221	237	240	19	(0.9)
19.	Tamil Nadu	285	297	311	311	319	34	(18.6)
20.	Uttar Pradesh	561	561	562	964	963	402	(11.9)
21.	West Bengal/Tripura Sikkim	348	348	357	372	374	26	(71.6)
22.	Delhi	55	57	57	57	57	2	(7.5)
23.	Pondicherry	—	—	2	11	14	14	(3.6)
	Total	4876	5640	5816	6504	6662	1786	(36.6)

Note: Figures within parenthesis against Col. 8 are the percentage increase during the period 1983-84 to 1987-88.

UC — University Colleges

AC — Affiliated Colleges

Source: Annual Report for the year 1988-89, University Grants Commission, New Delhi.

education than professional or technical education. This seem to indicate that in the regime of high rate of graduate unemployment in the country particularly of those who hold degrees in general higher education, the establishment[5] of non-professional colleges is unplanned and misconceived. This question however require further investigation, but the fact, for instance, is that the number of colleges in the country increased by 1351 during the period 1983-84 to 1987-88, mainly in the non-professional category (Table 2.3). The highest increase in number of colleges during this period has been recorded in the States Karnataka (516) followed by of UP (402). Other states where the increase was substantial were Madhya Pradesh (174), Maharashtra (172), Bihar (159), Andhra Pradesh (74) and Orissa (73). Table 2.4 provides statewise distribution of colleges in the country and increase in number of colleges in the last five years. It reveals that a few States, as above, have created more colleges than other States which partly explain the reasons for variations in educational efforts and achievements of the States due probably to their perception about the relative role in higher education in socio-economic progress.

In the Central sector, however, technical education which has been recognised as one of the most significant components of human resource development with great potential for adding value to products and services for uplifing the national economy and for improving the quality of life of people, was given greater emphasis as far as its expansion is concerned in the successive Five Year Plans. As a result, during the past four decades, there has been a phenomenal expansion of technical education facilities in the country. The number of institutions rose to 1300 in 1990-91 as compared to 111 in 1950-51, an increase by 12 times. Similarly, the enrolment increased from 55,000 in 1950-51 to 4,85,000 in 1990-91, i.e. an increase by about 8 times (Table 2.5). The state-wise break-up of technical institutions in the Central sector and enrolments are however not available for analysis.

Table 2.6 shows the extent and rate of increase in enrolment in higher education from 1950-51 to 1990-91. While the rate of increase has fluctuated from year to year between the range of 91.69 to 13.45 per cent; the overall growth in enrolment over the four decades has recorded an increase of twenty-five times or at the rate of about 10 per cent per annum. Of the total enrolment, undergraduate, postgraduate education and research accounted, in 1990-91, for 89.3, 9.6 and 1.1 per cent respectively (Table 2.7). A significant size, 83.4

TABLE 2.5: Progress of Technical Education in the Central Sector

	1950-51	1960-61	1970-71	1980-81	1990-91
I Engineering & Technological Colleges (Degree & above level)					
1. Number of Institutions	33	78	107	120	225
2. Enrolment in (000's)	17	48	93	130	182
II Engineering & Technological Colleges (Below degree level)					
1. Number of Institutions	78	130	631	885	1075
2. Enrolment (000's)	38	84	133	331	303
III (I + II)					
1. No. of Institutions	111	208	738	1005	1300
2. Enrolment (000's)	55	132	226	461	485

Source: Ministry of Human Resource Development Annual Report (1988-89), Govt. of India, New Delhi.

TABLE 2.6: Growth of Student Enrolment in Higher Education (1950-51 to 1990-91)

Years	Total Enrolment	Increase over proceeding five years	% increase over last five years
1	2	3	4
1950-51	173691	—	—
1955-56	294815	121124	69.73
1960-61	556559	261744	88.78
1965-66	1066884	510325	91.69
1970-71	1953700	886816	83.12
1975-76	2426109	472409	24.18
1980-81	2752437	326328	13.45
1985-86	3605029	852592	30.97
1990-91	4425247	820218	22.75

Source: Annual Reports for the years 1960-61 to 1990-91, University Grants Commission, New Delhi.

TABLE 2.7: Levelwise Enrolment in Higher Education (1950-51 to 1990-91)

Year	Undergraduate		Postgraduate		Research		Total Enrolment	
	No.	%	No.	%	No.	%	No.*	%
1	2	3	4	5	6	7	8	9
1950-51	145389	87.2	19992	12.0	1434	0.8	166815	100.00
1960-61	471658	88.0	58908	11.0	5083	1.0	535649	100.00
1970-71	1746090	90.0	161182	8.4	13311	0.7	1920583	100.00
1980-81	2401485	88.7	27337	10.1	32171	1.2	2706993	100.00
1990-91	3898643	89.3	420398	9.6	48678	1.1	4367719	100.00

* Total does not include the enrolment in Diploma and Certificate courses.

Source: Annual Reports of the University Grants Commission, New Delhi.

per cent, was enrolled in affiliated colleges, mainly at undergraduate level i.e. about 77 per cent of total enrolment (Table 2.8). The break-up of enrolment in the recent past by major faculties hardly indicate any significant shift in the balance towards professional courses (Table 2.9).

The enrolment ratio of female students is estimated to be 32.5 per cent, which varies a great deal across the States; the highest being 53 per cent for Kerala and the lowest of 16.4 per cent for Bihar of its total enrolment in 1990-91 (Table 2.10).

2.3 Teaching Staff in University Departments

Table 2.11 shows the strength and distribution of teaching staff in the university departments and university colleges during the period 1985-86 to 1990-91. In 1990-91 there were 58661 teachers in the university departments/constituent colleges. Out of these, (12.8 per cent) were professors, (26.2 per cent) readers, (57 per cent) lecturers and (4 per cent) tutors and demonstrators. Teaching staff in the university department/university colleges increased by 1929 in the year 1990-91 as compared to an increase of 2062 in the year 1986-87 over the preceding year. If the number of teachers in the affiliated colleges which comprise 78 per cent of the total teachers in higher education are also taken into account, the total number of teachers in that year would come to about 2.5 lakhs. The overall student-teacher ratio for higher education emerge to be 16 and the break-up of the ratio for the university departments and affiliated colleges is estimated to be 12 and 17, respectively.

2.4 Resources for Education

In view of the perceived need to enrich human resources especially by way of promoting education and training, the network of educational facilities are planned such that equity in the provision of such facilities and efficiency in delivery of services are duly ensured for various sections of the society. With a view to pursuing the social and economic goals of the country within the Constitutional framework, India has adopted a mixed economic system whereby Public sector has largely assumed the responsibility of providing infrastructural facilities, whereas the Private sector is to concentrate more on the mainstream of economic activities such as manufacturing

TABLE 2.8: Stagewise Enrolment: University Departments and Affiliated Colleges (1990-91)

Level of Education	University Deptts.	Affiliated Colleges	Total	% in Affiliated Colleges
1	2	3	4	5
Graduate	475634	3423009	3898643	77.3
	(64.9)	(92.7)	(88.1)	
Postgraduate	182873	237525	420398	5.4
	(25.0)	(6.4)	(9.5)	
Research	41376	7305	48678	0.2
	(5.7)	(0.2)	(1.1)	
Diploma/Certificate	32561	24967	57528	0.5
	(4.4)	(0.7)	(1.3)	
Total	732444	3692803	4425247	83.4
	(100.0)	(100.0)	(100.0)	

Source: Annual Report for the year 1990-91, University Grants Commission, New Delhi.

TABLE 2.9: Student Enrolment in Universities by Faculty (1985-86 to 1990-91)

S.No.	Course of	1985-86		1986-87		1987-88		1988-89		1989-90		1990-91	
		Enrolment	% of total	Enrolment	% of total	Enrolment	% of total	Enrolment	% of total	Enrolment	% of total	Enrolment	% of total
1	2	3	4	5	6	7	8	9	10	11	12	13	14
1.	Arts	1439071	40.3	1518282	40.4	1581542	40.4	1645414	40.4	1717437	40.4	178978	40.4
2.	Science	703467	19.7	735864	19.6	768022	19.6	800266	19.6	834087	19.6	869119	19.6
3.	Commerce	767743	21.5	822216	21.9	857971	21.9	893984	21.9	931765	21.9	969882	21.9
4.	Education	82131	2.3	86352	2.3	89949	2.3	93718	2.3	95979	2.3	99613	2.3
5.	Engineering & Technology	164261	4.6	183966	4.9	192148	4.9	201289	4.9	209371	4.9	216837	4.9
6.	Medicine	128552	3.6	127650	3.4	131013	3.4	137257	3.4	142270	3.4	150458	3.4
7.	Agriculture	46422	1.3	42800	1.1	43410	1.1	44007	1.1	45229	1.1	46908	1.1
8.	Veterinary Sci.	10713	0.3	9761	0.1	10168	0.3	10594	0.3	10957	0.3	11063	0.3
9.	Law	207112	5.8	198984	5.3	205318	5.3	213920	5.3	222961	5.3	234538	5.3
10.	Others	21425	0.6	28534	0.8	31287	0.8	34227	0.8	36822	0.8	37349	0.8
	Total	3570897	100.0	3754409	100.0	3910828	100.0	4074676	100.0	4246878	100.0	4425247	100.0

Source: Annual Report for the years 1989-90 and 1990-91, University Grants Commission, New Delhi.

TABLE 2.10: Women Enrolment in Higher Education by the States, 1990-91

S. No.	State/Union Territory	Total Enrolment	Women Enrolment	Percentage of Women
1	2	3	4	5
1.	Andhra Pradesh	305067	84504	27.7
2.	Assam	85797	26597	31.0
3.	Bihar	310672	50950	16.4
4.	Gujarat	263059	93123	35.4
5.	Haryana	93946	39645	42.2
6.	Himachal Pradesh	26016	6972	26.8
7.	Jammu & Kashmir	33298	12520	37.6
8.	Karnataka	290661	84873	29.2
9.	Kerala	167942	89003	53.0
10.	Madhya Pradesh	311836	106648	34.2
11.	Maharashtra	598519	220255	36.8
12.	Manipur	13469	4593	34.1
13.	Meghalaya/Mizoram/ Nagaland	12828	5003	39.0
14.	Orissa	93209	23302	25.0
15.	Punjab	161526	77856	48.2
16.	Rajasthan	202445	48992	24.4
17.	Tamil Nadul	393375	138381	38.5
18.	West Bengal	352238	135259	38.4
19.	Delhi	118536	54882	46.3
20.	Uttar Pradesh	590808	133523	22.6
	Total	4425247	1436887	32.5

Source: Annual Report for the year 1990-91, University Grants Commission, New Delhi.

and production of goods and services. In this mixed system, like the other sphere of development, the Private and Public sectors participate in extending the educational services at almost all levels and areas of specialisations. The responsibility for making adequate provision for educational facilities however, devolves mainly on the Government as even the private recognised institutions receive a considerably large proportion funds (about 55 per cent or so) from its

TABLE 2.11: Teaching Staff in the University Departments/Colleges (1985-86 to 1990-91)

Year	Professors	Readers	Lecturers	Tutors/ Demonstrators	Total
1	2	3	4	5	6
1985-86	5792	12026	29241	2029	49088
	(11.8)	(24.5)	(59.6)	(4.1)	(100.0)
1986-87	6445	13248	29360	2097	51150
	(12.6)	(25.9)	(57.4)	(4.1)	(100.0)
1987-88	6858	13982	30198	2127	53165
	(12.9)	(26.3)	(56.8)	(4.0)	(100.0)
1988-89	7037	14347	31390	2199	54973
	(12.8)	(26.1)	(57.1)	(4.0)	(100.0)
1989-90	7262	14864	32337	2269	56732
	(12.8)	(26.2)	(57.0)	(4.0)	(100.0)
1990-91	7509	15369	33437	2346	58661
	(12.8)	(26.2)	(57.0)	(4.0)	(100.0)

Source: Annual Report for the year 1990-91, University Grants Commission, New Delhi.

different agencies.

A large number of colleges are not on the grant list of the Government due mainly to their inability to satisfy the criteria for financial assistance stipulated by the funding agencies. The maintenance of standards of education however falls under the domain of the Government. Further, the responsibility of providing education is shared by various federating units of the Government—the Centre, the States and the local bodies. Till 1976, education was included in the States list of the Constitution and therefore, the States were largely responsible for the development of education while the Centre assumed a limited role in this regard. After the inclusion of education in the Concurrent list of the Constitution, education has become a joint responsibility of the Centre and the States; and, therefore, both the levels of governments are equally responsible for expediting the process of educational development by way of extending infrastructural facilities, providing necessary finance, monitoring of programmes through mutual cooperation and coordination of educational activities and maintenance of the standards of education. The costs of education are, thus, largely borne by both levels of the Governments—the Centre and the States—and partly by the individuals who benefit from education or buy education for their wards. The burden of financing education at all levels largely devolves on the States even though a multiple of agencies of the Centre are actively involved in promotion of higher education activities as is evident from the description of nature and types of universities in India and the methods of resource allocation for the promotion of higher education and research.

The universities and colleges are largely financed by the Central and the State Governments (about three-fourths) and the remaining portion is financed from fees, endowments and philanthropic contributions. The burden of financing higher education largely devolves on the States which contribute more than 80 per cent of the total expenditure. In addition, the Central Ministries like Agriculture, Industry and Human Resource Development, etc., directly extend financial assistance to universities which cater to their specific teaching and research requirements. The UGC, which is mainly responsibile for maintenance of standards of higher education and co-ordination of university activities, provides funds for the maintenance and development of the Central universities, all the Colleges in the Union Territory of Delhi and to about one-third of the 'deemed to be' universities also. The source of finance of the latter category of universities widely differ. There are those like Gujarat Vidyapith which are funded on the pattern of the Central universities which receive plan and non-plan grants from the UGC. A majority of institutions in this category are given almost the same treatment as the State universities which receive non-plan grants from the States while the plan grants are shared on matching basis between the States and the UGC. There is still another category of 'deemed to be' universities like Birla Institute of Technology and Science and Jamia Hamdard which do not receive plan and non-plan grants from the Government as they are fully dependent on private sources of financing. The Institutions of National Importance (INIs) like IITs are directly funded by the Department of Education of the Ministry of Human Resource Development. The States are responsible for meeting the entire non-plan expenditure of the institutions created by them while the UGC provides merely plan grants on matching basis to the State universities and colleges. The allocations made by the UGC across the States and type of institutions for plan and non-plan purposes greatly varies and show a bias in favour of Central universities and advanced States for different resources. As most of the institutions fall under the purview of the States, the finances for the development of higher education are largely provided by them from their own resources and partly from devolution of resources by the Centre through different channels of the Central government especially the Planning and Finance Commissions. The Central and the State Governments have thus entered into a meaningful partnership in providing financial sustenance to education system and their collective role determines the pace of development in the field of education.[6]

The relevant break-up of plan and non-plan expenditures by the Centre and the States may be seen in Table 2.12 which presents a detailed picture about the burden of financing education sector, including higher education on the Centre and the States in 1990-91. The following observations may be made: (a) The expenditure on higher education constituted merely 13.5 per cent of the total educational outlays; (b) The break up of plan and non-plan expenditure on higher education was 12 and 88 per cent, respectively; (c) The share of the Centre and the States in the total expenditure on higher education was 22 and 78 per cent respectively; and (d) The corresponding share in the plan expenditure alone was 55 and 45 per cent.

These are macro level statistics for the country as a whole, which obviously hide the extent of differences in allocation of funds for higher education across the Indian States. For instance, the estimates of average level of allocation for the entire seventh plan (1985-90) shows that whereas Andhra Pradesh spent as high as 20.5 per cent of the total educational outlay for higher education development, the corresponding share for Uttar Pradesh was as low as 8.3 per cent.

Obviously, a major portion of expenditure on universities comprises non-plan expenditure, which is fully borne by the States in respects of the institutions created by them. While some universities are provided funds on increamental basis in the form of block grants mainly in the range of 5 to 7 per cent over the previous level of expenditure, others receive funds on deficit basis, in the case of which entire expenditure on approved items are fully provided by the States. The method of assessment of financial requirement and the level of funding differ a great deal across the universities which also gets aggravated due to the following.

TABLE 2.12: Plan and Non-Plan Expenditure on Education System and Higher Education by the Centre and the States, 1990-91

(Rs. in crores)

Head of Expenditure	Education as a whole	Higher Education	Share of Higher Education in the total Educational Expenditure (%)
1	2	3	4
1. Plan Expenditure of which;	2272.64 (14.0)	269.60 (12.2)	11.9
2. Centre	918.30 (40.4)	147.60 (54.7)	16.1
3. States	1354.34 (59.6)	122.00 (45.3)	9.0
4. (2) %age of (1)	40.4	54.7	
1. Non-plan expenditure of which;	14017.58 (86.0)	1936.18 (87.8)	13.8
2. Centre	719.19 (5.1)	341.87 (17.7)	47.5
3. States	13298.39 (94.9)	1594.31 (82.3)	12.0
4. (2) as %age of (1)	5.1	17.1	
1. Total (Centre + State) of which;	16290.22 (100.0)	2205.78 (100.0)	13.5
2. Plan	2272.64 (100.0)	269.60 (100.0)	11.9
3. Non-Plan	14017.58 (100.0)	1936.18 (100.0)	13.8
4. (2) as %age of (1)	14.0	12.2	

Note: The figures in parenthesis indicate the percentage to the respective total.

Source: Department of Education, Ministry of Human Resource Development, Govt. of India.

As a measure of economy in expenditure there has been cuts almost in every plan period to the extent of 5 to 10 per cent or so by both the Central and the State governments in the non-plan expenditure. The persistence of inflationary pressure further erodes the already vulnerable financial base of universities. Since education budget constitutes about one fifth of the overall States' budget and a large part of it is on account of non-plan expenditure, education sector including higher education obviously suffers a great deal. As a result, the on-going programmes get hampered; affecting thereby, the quality and relevance of education. Since the universities are highly dependent on the Governments for funds, they experience acute difficulties in coping with the resource crunch as their abilities to exploit alternative sources of funds are limited due to several factors including the prevalent fiscal policy for the development of socio-economic sectors; which is structured to make the higher education institutions dependent on the Government. This is amply clear from the analysis of pattern of funding of select universities as discussed below.

2.5 Quantitative Dimensions of Selected Universities

A major purpose of the foregoing discussion has been to provide a brief background of the university system and the aspects of its financing in the country so that an objective appraisal of various dimensions of the select universities, especially the mechanisms of funding of these universities and the pattern of utilization of funds with respect to a wide range of chosen programmes, can be made.

2.5.1 Physical Expansion

All the universities in the sample were established between 1857 to 1968 and are therefore oldest in the country as already pointed out in Table 2.1. They offer programmes in a wide range of disciplines at all levels. Table 2.13 shows the number of departments under each faculty for all the universities. Evidently, the extent of diversification in terms of the large number of disciplines of study varies a great deal across the universities. An idea of the levels at which programmes are offered is obtained from Table 2.14 which indicate the size of enrolment and the respective shares in the total as well as at levels of postgraduate and undergraduate programmes. A significant majority of universities cater to postgraduate teaching and research. The enrolment ratios for Master's and degree courses also varies across the universities and so does the number of enrolment in science and technical based courses vis-a-vis arts and social sciences (Table 2.15). For the sample as a whole it emerges that 68 per cent of students were enrolled in humanities and social sciences whereas the

TABLE 2.13: Distribution of Departments by Faculty in Select Universities 1988-89

S.No.	Faculties	Anna-malai	BHU	Bombay	Cal-cutta	Delhi	Gauhati	HS Gaur	JNU*	Kerala	Kuruk-shetra	Madras	Mysore	Panjab	Utkal	Visva Bharati
1	2	3	4	5	6	7	8	9	10	11	12	13	14	15	16	17
1.	Arts (L)	17	40	21	22	24	19	17	5	21	22	34	19	29	10	28
2.	Commerce & Management	2	2	2	2	1	2	2	—	1	2	2	2	2	2	—
3.	Law	—	1	1	1	1	1	1	—	1	1	2	1	1	3	—
4.	Science	8	12	9	17	17	13	11	3	14	11	8	10	14	10	7
5.	Agriculture	6	11	—	1	—	—	—	—	—	—	—	—	—	—	11
6.	Engg. & Tech.	9	13	—	4	2	—	2	1	—	—	—	—	—	—	—
7.	Medical Science	3	28	—	—	2	—	1	—	—	—	1	—	—	—	—
	Total	45	107	33	47	47	35	34	9*	37	36	44	32	46	25	46

(—) Deptts. do not exist.

(L) Arts faculty: We have included here all the Deptts. concerned to Arts, fine arts, social sciences and humanities and languages to make it comparable.

*JNU: Science Faculty: included School of Comp. and systems sc., Environmental Scs.; School of Life Sci.,
Art Faculty: School of Int. Studies, School of languages, School of Physical Scs., School of Social Sciences, School of Arts and Aesthetics.
Engg. & Tech.: Centre for Bio-technology.

Source: Compiled from each university's Annual Reports 1988-89.

TABLE 2.14: Level-wise Enrolment Pattern in Select Universities 1988-89

S.No.	Faculties	Anna-malai	BHU*	Bombay	Cal-cutta	Delhi	Gauhati	HS Gaur	JNU	Kerala	Kuruk-shetra	Madras	Mysore	Panjab	Utkal	Visva Bharati
1	2	3	4	5	6	7	8	9	10	11	12	13	14	15	16	17
1.	Ph.D.	79 (1.0)	—	706 (10.9)	—	2466 (16.8)	335 (8.9)	284 (4.5)	—	864 (40.1)	83 (3.5)	1024 (34.8)	394 (6.7)	463 (8.6)	385 (14.0)	331 (11.9)
2.	M. Phil.	237 (3.0)	—	576 (8.9)	—	656 (4.5)	89 (2.4)	43 (0.7)	1546 (49.5)	131 (6.1)	254 (10.9)	397 (13.5)	3 (0.10)	337 (6.2)	195 (7.1)	—
3.	Post Graduate	2415 (30.6)	—	3201 (49.5)	—	6302 (42.9)	2637 (69.7)	1442 (23.0)	1296 (41.5)	883 (41.0)	1344 (57.6)	1209 (41.1)	2045 (34.9)	2269 (42.0)	2177 (78.9)	676 (24.3)
4.	Under Graduate	4884 (61.8)	—	1498 (23.2)	—	—	641 (16.9)	4485 (71.7)	NA	NA	478 (20.5)	NA	2670 (45.5)	1811 (33.5)	NA	1210 (43.6)
5.	Diploma	286 (3.6)	—	376 (5.8)	—	359 (2.4)	51 (1.3)	3 (0.05)	68 (2.2)	235 (10.9)	76 (3.3)	283 (9.6)	493 (8.4)	203 (3.8)	NA	158 (5.7)
6.	Certificate	—	—	107 (1.6)	—	4890 (33.3)	30 (0.8)	—	211 (6.8)	40 (1.8)	99 (4.2)	28 (1.0)	260 (4.4)	320 (5.9)	NA	402 (14.1)
	Total	7901 (100.0)	12919 (100.0)	6464 (100.0)	4196 (100.0)	14673 (100.0)	3783 (100.0)	6257 (100.0)	3121 (100.0)	2153 (100.0)	2334 (100.0)	2941 (100.0)	5865 (100.0)	5403 (100.0)	2757 (100.0)	2777 (100.0)

* — Level-wise enrolment is not available.

NA — Not Applicable.

Source: Compiled from Annual Report of the respective universities 1988-89

Note: Figures within parenthesis indicate the percentage to total.

TABLE 2.15: Science/Non-science Enrolment in Selected Universities, 1988-89

S. No.	University	Enrolment in Science Discipline	Enrolment in Non-science Discipline	Total
1	2	3	4	5
1.	Annamalai	5986 (75.76)	1915 (24.24)	7901
2.	BHU	4785 (37.04)	8134 (62.96)	12910
3.	Bombay	2303 (35.63)	4161 (64.37)	6464
4.	Calcutta	840 (20.02)	3356 (79.98)	4196
5.	Delhi	1998 (13.62)	12675 (86.38)	14673
6.	Gauhati	853 (22.55)	2930 (77.45)	3783
7.	HS Gaur	3200 (51.14)	3057 (48.86)	6257
8.	JNU	381 (12.21)	2740 (87.79)	3121
9.	Kerala	652 (30.28)	1501 (69.72)	2153
10.	Kurukshetra	597 (25.58)	1737 (74.42)	2334
11.	Madras	1168 (39.71)	1773 (60.29)	2334
12.	Mysore	766 (13.06)	5099 (66.94)	5865
13.	Panjab	1766 (32.68)	3637 (67.32)	5403
14.	Utkal	587 (21.29)	2170 (78.71)	2757
15.	Visva Bharati	736 (26.50)	2041 (73.50)	2777
	Total	26618 (31.86)	59926 (68.14)	83544 (100.0)

Source: Computed from the Annual Reports of each University for the year 1988-89.

Note: Figure in parenthesis indicate percentages to the total enrolment.

remaining 32 per cent were enrolled in science disciplines. The evidence thus demonstrates that these ratios are very close to the relevant percentage of science and non-science streams of students at the national level. These universities have a long way to go, indeed, towards orienting their programmes for promoting scientific and technical education which, in effect, determine productivity and production in every sphere of development.

Tables 2.16 and 2.17 present the break up of teaching and non-teaching staff at various levels in all the universities and shows the composition of teaching staff in select universities. It may be observed that *inter-se* percentages which vary so widely hardly lend any guidance about the ratios of senior teachers to the junior teachers or the ratios of senior university administrators to junior staff. In view of diverse university activities, it is however too early to conclude whether or not valid criteria are adopted to recruit and maintain staff positions in academic and non-academic disciplines in relation either to various levels of academic staff or students. We shall return to it later in Chapter 4, while analysing efficiency aspects of universities and the factors that contribute to it.

2.5.2 Finances

Of the various sources of income of universities, the income data for the universities are presented under the major items namely grants from the Governments, fees from students, examination fees, land property, library, sale proceeds, printing press, hostel charges, student services like games fees, etc. Table 2.18 demonstrates that financial dependence of these universities differ considerably. Among those which received more than 90 per cent of the total actual expenditure in 1988-89 from the Government sources are BHU, JNU and Visva Bharati. All of them are Central universities and they receive funds through UGC.

The universities which were dependent on the Government to the extent of 80 to 90 per cent in that year are: Calcutta (86.6 per cent), Delhi (89.1 per cent), Mysore (89.5 per cent) and Panjab (87.1 per cent). The universities which received less than 50 per cent of the expenditure as grant are Annamalai (29.8 per cent), Bombay (44.1 per cent), Madras (7.5 per cent) and Utkal (36.6 per cent). Clearly, the degree to which these universities have depended on the Government grants or have adopted other modes of funding from non-Government

TABLE 2.16: Composition of Teaching Staff in Select University, 1988-89

S. No.	Teaching Staff Position	Annamalai	BHU	Bombay	Calcutta	Delhi	Gauhati	HS Gaur	JNU	Kerala	Kurukshetra	Madras	Mysore	Panjab	Utkal	Visva Bharati
1	2	3	4	5	6	7	8	9	10	11	12	13	14	15	16	17
1.	Professor	83	253	64	—	154	61	51	71	65	59	78	98	168	56	33
		(14.3)	(19.5)	(19.4)		(25.7)	(16.2)	(17.1)	(20.1)	(26.7)	(19.1)	(18.6)	(14.9)	(21.6)	(20.0)	(17.3)
2.	Reader	140	535	101	—	232	147	116	119	66	118	106	155	282	95	61
		(24.2)	(41.3)	(30.6)		(38.7)	(39.1)	(38.8)	(33.8)	(27.2)	(38.2)	(25.3)	(23.6)	(36.3)	(33.8)	(31.9)
3.	Lecturer	355	507	144	—	187	149	117	143	81	127	209	392	268	108	91
		(61.4)	(39.2)	(43.6)		(31.2)	(39.6)	(39.1)	(40.6)	(33.3)	(41.1)	(49.9)	(59.7)	(34.5)	(38.4)	(47.6)
4.	Others	—	—	21	—	26	19	15	19	31	5	26	11	59	22	6
				(6.4)		(4.3)	(5.1)	(5.0)	(5.4)	(12.8)	(1.6)	(6.2)	(1.7)	(7.6)	(7.8)	(3.1)
	Total	578	1295	330	591	599	376	299	352	243	309	419	656	777	281	191
		(100.0)	(100.0)	(100.0)	(100.0)	(100.0)	(100.0)	(100.0)	(100.0)	(100.0)	(100.0)	(100.0)	(100.0)	(100.0)	(100.0)	(100.0)

Note: Figures within parenthesis indicate the percentage to total.

(—) Break up of teaching staff was not available.

Source: Compiled from Annual Reports of the respective universities, 1988-89.

TABLE 2.17: Break up of Non-Teaching Staff in Select Universities, 1988-89

S.No.	Status of Non-teaching staff	Annamalai	BHU	Bombay	Calcutta	Delhi	Gauhati	HS Gaur	JNU*	Kerala	Kurukshetra	Madras	Mysore	Panjab	Utkal	Visva Bharati
1	2	3	4	5	6	7	8	9	10	11	12	13	14	15	16	17
1.	Officers	—	154 (2.4)	29 (4.3)	—	40 (4.1)	—	4 (1.0)	11 (5.1)	33 (10.3)	2 (0.7)	—	29 (5.1)	95 (10.4)	—	—
2.	Ministerial	—	3132 (49.2)	441 (65.0)	—	496 (50.5)	95 (43.6)	160 (41.7)	172 (79.6)	147 (45.9)	160 (54.4)	180 (55.7)	214 (37.7)	464 (50.7)	109 (50.2)	—
3.	Class IV Staff	—	3085 (48.4)	208 (30.7)	—	435 (44.3)	122 (56.2)	220 (57.3)	33 (15.3)	140 (43.7)	125 (42.5)	143 (44.3)	310 (54.7)	356 (38.9)	108 (49.8)	—
4.	Others	—	—	—	—	11 (1.1)	—	—	—	—	7 (2.4)	—	14 (2.5)	—	—	—
	Total	—	6371 (100.0)	678 (100.0)	—	982 (100.0)	217 (100.0)	384 (100.0)	216 (100.0)	320 (100.0)	294 (100.0)	323 (100.0)	567 (100.0)	915 (100.0)	217 (100.0)	—

Note: Figures within parenthesis indicate the percentage to total.

(—) Break up is not available.

Source: Compiled from annual Reports of the Respective universities, 1988-89.

TABLE 2.18: Sources of Income in Select Universities, 1988-89

(Rs. in Lakhs)

S.No.	Faculties	Anna-malai	BHU	Bombay	Cal-cutta	Delhi	Gauhati	HS Gaur	JNU*	Kerala	Kuruk-shetra	Madras	Mysore	Panjab	Utkal	Visva Bharati
1	2	3	4	5	6	7	8	9	10	11	12	13	14	15	16	17
1.	Grants	101.12 (29.8)	3297.20 (91.5)	466.34 (44.1)	1200.00 (86.6)	1813.31 (89.1)	250.60 (58.3)	250.36 (50.1)	953.32 (95.7)	504.55 (57.5)	522.00 (73.9)	96.81 (7.5)	678.57 (89.5)	1457.5 (87.1)	188.97 (36.6)	751.13 (97.4)
2.	Fees from Students	—	23.21 (0.6)	133.73 (12.6)	18.95 (1.4)	51.91 (2.6)	—	12.08 (2.4)	6.13 (0.6)	—	—	96.50 (7.5)	19.04 (2.5)	13.81 (0.8)	16.62 (3.2)	5.53 (0.6)
3.	Examination Fees	109.63 (32.3)	11.64 (0.3)	231.71 (21.9)	142.17 (10.3)	115.94 (5.7)	148.35 (34.5)	137.12 (27.5)	—	230.32 (26.2)	115.81 (16.4)	254.32 (19.7)	—	126.62 (7.6)	—	—
4.	Land Property	8.84 (2.6)	9.53 (0.3)	—	—	—	2.49 (0.6)	5.87 (1.2)	19.45 (2.0)	—	6.40 (0.9)	3.97 (0.3)	15.13 (2.0)	—	—	2.80 (0.4)
5.	Library	—	—	0.72 (0.1)	—	—	—	0.40 (0.1)	—	—	—	—	—	1.77 (0.1)	—	—
6.	Sale Proceed	1.87 (0.6)	2.27 (0.1)	1.69 (0.2)	6.87 (0.5)	2.8 (0.1)	12.17 (2.8)	2.34 (0.5)	0.16 (0.02)	—	3.99 (0.6)	4.33 (0.3)	6.67 (1.0)	1.49 (0.1)	—	0.42 (0.05)
7.	Printing Press	—	—	31.07 (2.9)	—	—	—	20.08 (4.0)	—	—	23.00 (3.2)	—	—	5.28 (0.3)	—	—
8.	Hostels	—	6.93 (0.2)	6.58 (0.6)	—	—	—	1.23 (0.2)	4.00 (0.4)	2.38 (0.3)	3.51 (0.5)	—	—	0.76 (0.5)	—	1.62 (0.2)

(Contd.)

TABLE 2.18 *(Contd.)*

1	2	3	4	5	6	7	8	9	10	11	12	13	14	15	16	17
9.	Student Services	—	—	—	3.28 (0.21)	—	—	—	—	—	—	—	—	—	—	—
10.	Miscellaneous	—	46.41 (1.31)	82.73 (7.8)	5.61 (0.4)	26.0 (1.3)	1.99 (0.5)	—	13.20 (1.3)	20.22 (2.3)	22.59 (3.2)	243.17 (18.8)	35.24 (4.6)	51.75 (3.1)	4.59 (0.9)	6.20 (0.8)
11.	Others	117.89 (34.7)	206.33 (5.7)	103.36 (9.8)	9.60 (0.7)	24.9 (1.2)	14.26 (3.3)	69.67 (14.0)	—	120.09 (13.7)	9.41 (1.3)	591.73 (45.8)	3.48 (0.5)	14.52 (0.9)	305.82 (59.3)	4.42 (0.6)
	Total	339.35 (100.0)	3603.52 (100.0)	1057.93 (100.0)	1386.48 (100.0)	2034.86 (100.0)	429.86 (100.0)	499.15 (100.0)	996.26 (100.0)	877.56 (100.0)	706.41 (100.0)	1290.83 (100.0)	758.13 (100.0)	1673.5 (100.0)	516.0 (100.0)	771.12 (100.0)

Note : Figure within parenthesis are the percentages to total.

Others — Included income from transfer payments, recoveries, donations from other bodies and Associations and income from Cultural & Sports competitions.

(—) break up is not available.

Source: Computed from "Financial Estimates" of the universities, 1990-91.

sources varies a grant deal across the universities.

The second most important source of income has been the examination fees, particularly with respect to affiliating universities as may be seen in the table referred to above. The collections from other sources particularly for the universities of Annamalai, Madras, and Utkal being 34.7, 45.8 and 59.3 per cent, respectively, are too high which are attributable largely to generation of revenues from the programmes of correspondence courses.[7]

The collection of fees including tuition fees accounts for a very small share of the total fees, below 5 per cent in almost all the universities except Bombay (12.6 per cent) and Madras (7.5 per cent). The collection of hostel charges is less than one per cent even for such a major residential university as BHU (0.2 per cent) and JNU (0.4 per cent). It follows that:

(i) the Central universities are more dependent on the Government than the State universities;
(ii) the State universities, mainly of affiliating type, are dependent on income from both the Government sources as well as fees from conduct of examination and programmes of distance education, whenever applicable;
(iii) the extent of augmentation of resources from non-Government sources widely varies as much as they vary in their relative dependence on Government funds; and
(iv) the revenue raising policies and practices of different universities is so diverse that there is seemingly much scope for them to benefit from each other's experiences to shift the balance of financial dependence in a desirable direction.

In the following paragraphs, an attempt is made to examine as to how the revenues, thus, raised are allotted by the universities for various purposes.

2.5.3 Pattern of Utilization of Funds

An analysis of time-series data pertaining to the utilization of funds by universities in India reveal that about 56 per cent of the total expenditure is spent on payment of salaries of teaching (32 per cent) and non-teaching staff (24 per cent). The remaining share is spent on non-salary items, including equipment and appliances and library which together account for 10 to 12 per cent.[8] As against this, the payment of salaries for the group of 15 universities accounted for 66 per cent in 1988-89, of which 25 and 41 per cent was incurred on account of salaries of teaching and non-teaching staff, respectively. As compared to the average for the entire university system in India, the payment of salaries to non-teaching staff for the group is considerably high. The respective position of individual university vis-a-vis others differ a great deal as may be observed in Table 2.19, which presents the break-up of expenditure under the broad categories of academic and the central administrative functions; and under each of these two major heads the relevant disaggregated figures for salary and non-salary items are also shown.

2.5.3.1 Analysis of Expenditure: An Aggregative (i.e. Institutional) Level

As discussed before, the funds are acquired by educational institutions from multiple of sources in varying proportions. The resources provided by funding agencies mainly in the form of block grants are not earmarked for specific purposes and therefore receipient institutions enjoy considerable autonomy in allocation of funds for various academic and related activities. But the recurring and non-recurring expenditures have to be incurred for the approved programmes as sanctioned by the funding agencies. In order to determine the magnitude of funds required by an institution for its operational and development purposes, it is important to analyse and examine the relevant data to deal with such questions as: What amount of money is spent on various activities? How much it costs the institution to maintain the given number of seats in various courses? How much of its total resources go into the creation of additional facilities or faculties and with what results? With a view to obtaining an idea about these questions and the related issues, it is imperative to study the structure of university finances, before attempting estimation of unit costs of education as obtaining in different institutions for various programmes.

The recurring expenditure has been examined under six major heads, namely, expenditure on teaching staff, administration, common services, student services, library services and examination. The non-recurring expenditure is considered under four broad categories of expenditure, namely, building, furniture, equipment and books.

TABLE 2.19: Recurring Expenditure by Major Components 1988-89

S. No.	Major Components of Expenditure	Annamalai	BHU	Bombay	Calcutta	Delhi	Gauhati	HS Gaur	JNU*	Kerala	Kurukshetra	Madras	Mysore	Panjab	Utkal	Visva Bharati	Mean	S.D.	C.V. (%)
1	2	3	4	5	6	7	8	9	10	11	12	13	14	15	16	17	18	19	20
Academic Expenses																			
1.	Salary & Allowances of Teaching Staff	235.4 (29.0)	1049.7 (27.6)	154.6 (13.1)	364.7 (37.4)	485.5 (27.3)	119.9 (24.6)	109.9 (23.3)	250.1 (24.3)	137.9 (14.3)	162.0 (21.5)	158.9 (15.6)	236.4 (29.9)	483.8 (28.2)	112.8 (21.8)	211.9 (33.6)	284.9 (25.2	236.6	83
2.	Salary & Allowances of Non-Teaching Staff	70.4 (8.7)	703.2 (18.5)	173.5 (14.7)	139.4 (14.2)	237.8 (13.4)	38.5 (7.9)	74.3 (15.7)	27.0 (2.6)	51.4 (5.3)	50.8 (6.8)	78.8 (7.7)	78.8 (10.0)	192.8 (11.2)	42.2 (8.1)	47.8 (7.6)	133.8 (11.9)	164.0	123
3.	Non-Salary items	128.2 (15.8)	181.5 (4.8)	101.5 (8.6)	73.8 (7.6)	90.1 (5.1)	11.8 (2.4)	26.0 (5.5)	64.5 (6.3)	23.7 (2.5)	19.9 (2.6)	52.4 (5.2)	10.5 (1.3)	248.7 (14.6)	16.7 (3.2)	26.2 (4.1)	71.7 (6.4)	67.2	94
4.	Sub Total (1+2+3)	434.0 (53.5)	1934.4 (50.8)	429.6 (36.4)	577.9 (59.2)	813.4 (45.8)	170.2 (34.9)	210.2 (44.5)	341.6 (33.2)	213.0 (22.1)	232.7 (30.9)	290.1 (28.5)	325.7 (41.2)	925.3 (54.0)	171.7 (33.1)	285.9 (45.3)	490.4 (43.5)	443.5	90
Central Adm. and Common Services																			
5.	Salary & Allowances of Non-Teaching Staff	88.7 (10.9)	942.7 (24.7)	415.8 (35.2)	368.7 (37.8)	503.7 (28.4)	214.4 (43.9)	117.2 (24.8)	233.8 (22.7)	411.5 (42.7)	312.0 (41.5)	191.9 (18.8)	235.8 (29.8)	503.4 (29.3)	171.7 (33.1)	231.2 (36.7)	329.5 (29.2)	206.6	63
6.	Non-Salary items	289.9 (35.7)	931.4 (24.4)	336.3 (28.4)	29.1 (3.0)	458.5 (25.8)	103.4 (21.2)	144.7 (30.7)	452.2 (44.0)	338.0 (35.2)	207.0 (27.5)	537.3 (57.2)	228.9 (29.0)	286.0 (16.7)	174.5 (33.7)	113.0 (17.9)	308.7 (27.3)	216.9	70

(Contd.)

TABLE 2.19 *(Contd.)*

1	2	3	4	5	6	7	8	9	10	11	12	13	14	15	16	17	18	19	20
7.	Sub-Total (5+6)	378.6 (46.6)	1874.1 (49.2)	752.1 (63.6)	397.8 (40.8)	962.2 (54.2)	317.8 (65.1)	261.9 (55.5)	686.0 (66.7)	749.5 (77.9)	519.0 (69.0)	729.2 (71.5)	464.7 (58.8)	789.4 (46.0)	346.2 (66.8)	344.2 (54.6)	638.2 (56.5)	389.9	61
	Grand Total (4+7)	812.6 (100.0)	3808.5 (100.0)	1181.7 (100.0)	975.7 (100.0)	1775.6 (100.0)	488.0 (100.0)	472.1 (100.0)	1027.6 (100.0)	962.5 (100.0)	751.7 (100.0)	1019.3 (100.0)	790.4 (100.0)	1714.7 (100.0)	517.9 (100.0)	630.1 (100.0)	1128.6 (100.0)	809.9	72

Note :Figures within parenthesis are the percentages to Grand Total.

S.D. = Standard Deviation

C.V. = Coefficient of Variation

Source: Computed from Financial Estimates of the Respective Universities, 1990-91.

Of the total recurring expenditure for the fifteen universities, on an average, 43.5 per cent was incurred on the academic activities including payment of salaries of other supporting activities. The remaining 56.5 per cent of the total expenditure accounted for central expenditure which includes salaries of non-teaching staff and other expenses incurred by the Central administrative units (Col. 18 of Table 2.19). The share of salaries of teaching staff alone was marely 25 per cent. In the sample of universities, whereas University of Calcutta spent a maximum of 59.2 per cent on academic activities, University of Kerala incurred as low as 22.1 per cent of the total recurring expenditure. There are, thus, considerable differences in allocation of resources by universities for academic and other supporting services, which is duly revealed by the high Co-efficient of Variation (CV) (90 per cent). At the dis-aggregated level also, considerable variations are observed with respect to all the heads of expenditure across the observed with respect to all the heads of expenditure across the universities. For instance, payment of salaries to teaching staff constitutes a major share for University of Calcutta (37.4 per cent). The corresponding share for University of Bombay being 13.1 per cent is the minimum in the sample.

Among the various components of expenditure, variations in the payment of salaries to the non-teaching staff attached to academic departments has emerged highest, the estimated CV being 123 per cent. As against the average payment of 11.9 per cent, the respective share for BHU was as high as 18.5 per cent whereas the corresponding share for JNU was as low as 2.6 per cent. It may be noted that these extreme situation lies in the Central universities, which are funded by the single agency i.e. UGC.

The expenses incurred by teaching departments under non-salary heads include laboratory equipment, consumables, stationary and other teaching materials, which are necessary for supporting teaching activities. On an average, the expenditure under this category accounted for 6.4 per cent of the total recurring expenditure. While the maximum (15.8 per cent) expenditure on this account was incurred by Annamalai University, the Mysore University spent as low as 1.3 per cent.

The central administrative expenditure which accounted for 56.5 per cent of the total recurring expenditure includes two major components i.e. salary of non-academic staff and non-salary expenses like maintenance of building and other infrastructure facilities including consumables. The salary component of central expenditure was 29.2 per cent; the maximum being 43.9 per cent for Gauhati University. Further, the average non-salary expenses of the central expenditure was worked out at 27.3 per cent of the total expenditure the highest and lowest being 44 and 3 per cent, respectively, for JNU and Calcutta University.

In all, of the total expenditure, 66.3 per cent was spent by the sampled universities on the payment of salaries of teaching (25.2 per cent) and non-teaching staff (41.1 per cent) and the remaining share was accounted for by non-salary items of expenditure. While there are university to university variations, as indicated above, these ratios are very close to the national averages.

2.5.3.2 Analysis of Expenditure at Disaggregative (i.e. Faculty) Level

As mentioned earlier, the expenditure incurred by universities could be classified under broad two categories: teaching and non-teaching expenditure including the expenditure on common services. In the following paragraphs faculty-wise expense on teaching are discussed so as to obtain an idea of allocation pattern across the institutions. The expenditure by Central Administration would be discussed separately. Table 2.20 summarises the faculty-wise total expenditure of the fifteen universities. The distribution of teaching expenditure among the faculties obviously varies due to the relative emphasis of each university on different programmes. The results are self-explanatory as shown in the above mentioned Table 2.20. They are therefore, not discussed here. It would however be worthwhile to discuss the pattern of allocation under broad heads of expenditure for major faculties, which are comparable.

2.5.3.2.1 Faculty of Arts

The recurring expenditure of the faculty has been determined by taking into account (i) salary and allowances of teaching staff; (ii) salary and allowances of non-teaching supporting staff; and, (iii) non-salary items of expenditures. All the departments which fall under the faculty are covered. The relevant data as provided in the university budgets have been clubbed together, to reflect the total expenditure under different categories. The pattern of recurring expenditure shows that the salary and allowances constitute a major part of the total expenditure. Table 2.21 presents the absolute and

TABLE 2.20: Recurring Expenditure by Faculties

(Rs. in lakhs)

S. No.	Universities	Faculties							Total
		Arts	Science	Comm. & Mgt.	Law	Engg. & Tech.	Medical	Agriculture	
1	2	3	4	5	6	7	8	9	10
1.	Annamalai	65.93 (15.2)	58.20 (13.4)	10.08 (2.3)	—	71.86 (16.5)	195.0 (44.9)	32.96 (7.6)	433.86 (100.0)
2.	BHU	311.75 (17.5)	305.15 (17.2)	37.51 (2.1)	23.52 (1.3)	430.62 (24.2)	569.02 (32.0)	98.89 (5.7)	1776.46 (100.0)
3.	Bombay	97.96 (22.8)	288.63 (67.2)	37.78 (8.8)	5.27 (1.2)	—	—	—	429.64 (100.0)
4.	Calcutta	145.91 (25.2)	301.54 (52.2)	14.31 (2.5)	5.01 (0.9)	91.98 (15.9)	—	19.2 (3.3)	577.95 (100.0)
5.	Delhi	343.9 (42.2)	342.0 (42.0)	42.9 (5.3)	74.7 (9.2)	0.1 (0.01)	9.8 (1.2)	—	813.4 (100.0)
6.	Gauhati	57.60 (33.8)	96.43 (56.7)	9.45 (5.6)	6.68 (3.9)	—	—	—	170.16 (100.0)
7.	HS Gaur	54.84 (26.1)	111.96 (53.2)	6.23 (3.9)	4.01 (0.02)	14.14 (6.7)	17.15 (8.1)	—	210.23 (100.0)
8.	JNU	236.63 (70.2)	92.65 (27.5)	—	—	7.72 (2.3)	—	—	337.0 (100.0)

(Contd.)

TABLE 2.20 (*Contd.*)

1	2	3	4	5	6	7	8	9	10
9.	Kerala	93.61 (44.0)	97.26 (45.7)	21.63 (10.1)	0.49 (0.2)	—	—	—	212.99 (100.0)
10.	Kurukshetra	103.67 (44.5)	100.34 (42.2)	15.60 (6.7)	13.06 (5.6)	—	—	—	232.67 (100.0)
11.	Madras	93.58 (32.3)	152.06 (52.4)	8.31 (2.9)	4.14 (1.4)	—	32.0 (11.4)	—	290.09 (100.0)
12.	Mysore	98.29 (44.9)	87.37 (39.9)	30.12 (13.8)	3.14 (1.4)	—	—	—	218.92 (100.0)
13.	Panjab	271.41 (31.2)	561.57 (64.7)	5.37 (0.6)	30.8 (3.5)	—	—	—	868.43 (100.0)
14.	Utkal	55.87 (32.5)	84.73 (49.2)	6.02 (3.5)	25.75 (13.8)	—	—	—	172.37 (100.0)
15.	Visva Bharati	127.70 (44.6)	56.25 (19.7)	48.26 (16.9)	—	—	—	53.75 (18.8)	285.86 (100.0)
	Average	143.9 (23.3)	182.4 (29.5)	29.7 (3.5)	16.32 (2.6)	38.2 (6.2)	164.6 (26.6)	52.2 (8.3)	617.7 (100.0)

Note: Figures within the parenthesis are the percentages to total.

relative level of expenditure.

As may be seen in Table 2.21 that payment of salaries to teaching staff has emerged, as may be expected, a dominant share (73.5 per cent) in the total faculty's expenditure; though *inter-se* percentages have varied between 53 to 89 per cent. The corresponding share of non-teaching staff was 19.5 per cent, while the expenditure on non-salary items, mainly stationary, and other expenses was 7 per cent. In brief, while there are considerable variations in labour intensity of faculties of Arts across the universities as measured by payment of salaries to staff, on an average, the disciplines of studies under the Faculty of Arts are highly labour intensive to the extent of 93 per cent.

2.5.3.2.2 Faculty of Science

Unlike the pattern of expenditure of Faculty of Arts where teaching staff salary emerged a major component of total expenditure, the Faculty of Science (Table 2.22) reveal a somewhat different pattern in so far as relative level of expenditure on salary and non-salary items are concerned. On an average, 50.8 per cent of the total expenditure was incurred on payment of salary of teaching staff, followed by the salary of non-teaching staff (28.8 per cent) and non-salary expenses (21 per cent). Inter-university comparisons reveals a divergent trend. For instance, there is only one university, namely Bombay, where non-teaching staff salary (41.4 per cent) was higher than salary of teaching staff (32 per cent). The share of teaching staff salary for Annamalai University is observed highest (76.3 per cent), but non-salary expenditure was as low as 6.1 per cent of the total faculty expenditure. Likewise, JNU incurred the highest share on non-salary items (43.4 per cent) and the lowest on non-teaching staff salary (6.6 per cent). Inspite of differences in allocation of resources on salary and non-salary items, the share of expenditure on technical/ supporting staff, equipment and other consumable items was almost 50 per cent, which is, as may be expected, much higher than that of Arts Facultry.

2.5.3.2.3 Faculty of Commerce and Management

Like the Faculty of Arts, the teaching staff salary component has emerged nearly three-fourths of total expenditure for this faculty

TABLE 2.21: Recurring Expenditure by Major Components, 1988-89 (Faculty of Arts)

(Rs. in lakhs)

S. No.	Universities	Salary & Allowances		Non-Salary Items	Total
		Teaching Staff	Non-Teaching Staff		
1	2	3	4	5	6
1.	Annamalai	59.0 (89.5)	5.0 (7.6)	1.93 (2.9)	65.93 (100.0)
2.	BHU	244.01 (78.3)	63.45 (20.3)	4.29 (1.4)	311.75 (100.0)
3.	Bombay	52.35 (53.4)	33.87 (34.6)	11.74 (12.0)	97.96 (100.0)
4.	Calcutta	107.26 (73.5)	33.0 (22.6)	5.65 (3.9)	145.91 (100.0)
5.	Delhi	230.9 (67.2)	83.0 (24.1)	30.0 (8.7)	343.9 (100.0)
6.	Gauhati	48.68 (84.6)	7.86 (13.6)	1.06 (1.8)	57.60 (100.0)
7.	HS Gaur	36.03 (65.7)	15.80 (28.8)	3.01 (5.5)	54.84 (100.0)
8.	JNU	200.29 (84.7)	19.72 (8.3)	16.62 (7.0)	236.43 (100.0)
9.	Kerala	64.75 (69.2)	24.39 (26.0)	4.47 (4.8)	93.61 (100.0)
10.	Kurukshetra	72.99 (70.4)	18.16 (17.5)	12.52 (12.1)	103.67 (100.0)
11.	Madras	62.47 (66.8)	21.54 (23.0)	9.55 (10.2)	93.56 (100.0)
12.	Mysore	74.29 (75.6)	21.72 (22.1)	2.28 (2.3)	98.29 (100.0)
13.	Panjab	175.67 (64.7)	56.21 (20.7)	39.53 (14.6)	271.41 (100.0)
14.	Utkal	49.90 (89.3)	1.56 (2.8)	4.41 (7.9)	55.87 (100.0)
15.	Visva Bharati	107.53 (84.2)	15.23 (11.9)	4.94 (3.9)	127.7 (100.0)
	Average	105.7 (73.5)	28.0 (19.5)	10.1 (7.0)	143.8 (100.0)

Note : Figures within the parenthesis are the percentages to total.

TABLE 2.22: Recurring Expenditure by Major Components, 1988-89 (Faculty of Science)

(Rs. in lakhs)

S. No.	Universities	Salary & Allowances		Non-Salary Items	Total
		Teaching Staff	Non-Teaching Staff		
1	2	3	4	5	6
1.	Annamalai	44.38 (76.3)	10.25 (17.6)	3.57 (6.1)	58.20 (100.0)
2.	BHU	170.91 (56.0)	97.76 (32.0)	36.48 (12.0)	305.15 (100.0)
3.	Bombay	92.25 (32.0)	119.49 (41.4)	76.89 (26.6)	288.63 (100.0)
4.	Calcutta	189.79 (62.9)	64.77 (21.5)	46.98 (15.6)	301.54 (100.0)
5.	Delhi	171.9 (50.3)	120.6 (35.3)	49.5 (14.4)	342.0 (100.0)
6.	Gauhati	60.35 (62.6)	26.81 (27.8)	9.27 (9.6)	96.43 (100.0)
7.	HS Gaur	54.00 (48.3)	41.00 (36.6)	16.86 (15.1)	111.86 (100.0)
8.	JNU	46.31 (50.0)	6.14 (6.6)	40.2 (43.4)	92.65 (100.0)
9.	Kerala	52.33 (53.8)	26.14 (26.9)	18.79 (19.3)	97.26 (100.0)
10.	Kurukshetra	67.76 (67.5)	26.02 (25.9)	6.56 (6.6)	100.34 (100.0)
11.	Madras	72.50 (47.7)	43.28 (28.5)	36.28 (23.8)	152.06 (100.0)
12.	Mysore	54.18 (62.0)	26.59 (30.4)	6.60 (7.6)	87.37 (100.0)
13.	Panjab	232.64 (41.4)	125.0 (22.3)	203.93 (36.3)	561.57 (100.0)
14.	Utkal	46.07 (54.4)	29.50 (34.8)	9.16 (10.8)	84.73 (100.0)
15.	Visva Bharati	35.64 (63.4)	8.83 (15.7)	11.78 (20.9)	56.25 (100.0)
	Average	92.7 (50.8)	51.5 (28.2)	38.2 (21.0)	182.4 (100.0)

Note : Figures within the parenthesis are the percentages to total.

(Table 2.23). The average shares of payment of salaries of teaching, non-teaching staff and non-salary emerged 74.3, 17.6 and 8.1 per cent, respectively. The universities which incurred the highest amount on salaries of teaching staff are Kerala (95.7 per cent), BHU (95.4 per cent), and Annamalai (91.7 per cent). At the lower end are University of Bombay (19.3 per cent), Gauhati (58.1 per cent) and HS Gaur (65.6 per cent). In the category of non-teaching staff, the University of Bombay spent (47.4 per cent). The lowest non-teaching staff salary and non-salary expenses were estimated for Annamalai (3.5 per cent) and BHU (0.4 per cent), respectively. The University of Bombay not only spent a lower share of the total expenditure on teaching staff salary (19.3 per cent) as compared to non-teaching staff (47.4 per cent) but non-salary expenses of this faculty was as high as 33.3 per cent. The causes of such variations would be explored later.

2.5.3.2.4 Faculty of Law

The different components of total expenditure of faculty of law is shown in Table 2.24 for the select universities. The average level of payment of salaries of teaching, non-teaching staff and non-salary items are worked out to be 69.6, 25.2 and 5.2 per cent, respectively. Teaching staff salary emerged highest in BHU (97.6 per cent) while minimum was (30.6 per cent) for University of Kerala. In University of Kerala, the share of non-salary expenses was highest (57.2 per cent). In Bombay University non-teaching staff salary was as high as 42.5 per cent, while for Gauhati University it was as low as 10.3 per cent of the total expenditure.

2.5.3.3 Central Expenditure

The expenditure incurred by the central administration and common services constitutes a major portion of the total expenditure in each university, the absolute and relative level however varies from 41 to 78 per cent (Table 2.19) of the total recurring expenditure. Table 2.25 summarises the central expenditure under six major heads, namely, general administration, common services, student services, examination, labrary and institutions maintained by University. The various items of expenditure included under each of these heads are indicated in Section 3.2.4 of Chapter 3 where we have discussed unit costs of these services. Of the total central expenditure, on an

TABLE 2.23: Recurring Expenditure by Major Components, 1988-89
(Faculty of Commerce and Management)

(Rs. in lakhs)

S. No.	Universities	Salary & Allowances		Non-Salary Items	Total
		Teaching Staff	Non-Teaching Staff		
1	2	3	4	5	6
1.	Annamalai	9.24 (91.7)	0.35 (3.5)	0.49 (4.8)	10.08 (100.0)
2.	BHU	35.77 (95.4)	1.58 (4.2)	0.16 (0.4)	37.51 (100.0)
3.	Bombay	7.28 (19.3)	17.92 (47.4)	12.58 (33.3)	37.78 (100.0)
4.	Calcutta	11.86 (82.9)	1.54 (10.8)	0.91 (6.3)	14.31 (100.0)
5.	Delhi	30.4 (70.9)	10.0 (23.3)	2.5 (5.8)	42.9 (100.0)
6.	Gauhati	5.49 (58.1)	3.15 (33.3)	0.81 (8.6)	9.45 (100.0)
7.	HS Gaur	5.40 (65.6)	2.45 (29.8)	0.38 (4.6)	8.23 (100.0)
8.	Kerala	20.69 (95.7)	0.83 (3.8)	0.11 (0.5)	21.63 (100.0)
9.	Kurukshetra	11.95 (76.6)	2.96 (19.0)	0.69 (4.4)	15.60 (100.0)
10.	Madras	5.80 (69.8)	2.14 (25.8)	0.37 (0.37)	8.31 (100.0)
11.	Mysore	5.16 (85.7)	0.79 (13.1)	0.07 (1.2)	6.02 (100.0)
12.	Panjab	21.86 (72.6)	5.48 (18.2)	2.78 (9.2)	30.12 (100.0)
13.	Utkal	3.69 (68.8)	0.99 (18.4)	0.69 (12.8)	5.37 (100.0)
14.	Visva Bharati	44.48 (92.2)	2.16 (4.5)	1.62 (3.3)	48.26 (100.0)
	Average	15.6 (74.3)	3.7 (17.6)	1.7 (8.1)	21.0 (100.0)

Note : Figures within the parenthesis are the percentages to total.

TABLE 2.24: Recurring Expenditure by Major Components, 1988-89 (Faculty of Law)

(Rs. in lakhs)

S. No.	Universities	Salary & Allowances		Non-Salary Items	Total
		Teaching Staff	Non-Teaching Staff		
1	2	3	4	5	6
1.	BHU	22.96 (97.6)	—	0.56 (2.4)	23.52 (100.0)
2.	Bombay	2.70 (51.2)	2.24 (42.5)	0.33 (6.3)	5.27 (100.0)
3.	Calcutta	3.69 (73.6)	—	1.32 (26.4)	5.01 (100.0)
4.	Delhi	52.3 (70.0)	20.6 (27.6)	1.8 (2.4)	74.7 (100.0)
5.	Gauhati	5.36 (80.3)	0.69 (10.3)	0.63 (9.4)	6.68 (100.0)
6.	HS Gaur	2.26 (56.3)	1.44 (35.9)	0.31 (7.8)	4.01 (100.0)
7.	Kerala	0.15 (30.6)	0.06 (12.2)	0.28 (57.2)	0.49 (100.0)
8.	Kurukshetra	9.29 (71.1)	3.62 (27.7)	0.15 (1.2)	13.06 (100.0)
9.	Madras	3.22 (77.4)	0.88 (21.1)	0.06 (1.5)	4.16 (100.0)
10.	Mysore	2.64 (84.1)	0.35 (11.1)	0.15 (4.8)	3.14 (100.0)
11.	Panjab	21.57 (71.7)	6.08 (20.2)	2.43 (8.1)	30.08 (100.0)
12.	Utkal	13.18 (51.2)	10.16 (39.5)	2.41 (9.3)	25.75 (100.0)
	Average	11.61 (69.6)	4.61 (25.2)	0.87 (5.2)	16.32 (100.0)

Notes : Figures within the parenthesis are the percentages to total.
— Figures are not reported in the budget.

TABLE 2.25: Recurring Expenditure by Functions
(Central Administration & Common Services)

(Rs. in lakhs)

S. No.	Universities	Adminis-tration	Common Services	Student Services	Exami-nation	Library	Univ. main-tained institutions	Total
1	2	3	4	5	6	7	8	9
1.	Annamalai	51.91 (13.7)	72.68 (19.2)	170.43 (17.2)	65.21 (17.2)	8.89 (2.3)	9.52 (2.6)	378.64 (100.0)
2.	BHU	360.79 (18.6)	638.92 (33.0)	198.54 (10.2)	63.71 (3.3)	73.78 (3.8)	602.93 (31.1)	1938.67 (100.0)
3.	Bombay	260.0 (34.6)	221.87 (29.5)	50.66 (6.7)	145.24 (19.3)	51.04 (6.8)	23.27 (3.1)	752.08 (100.0)
4.	Calcutta	132.47 (33.3)	104.56 26.3)	49.73 (12.5)	75.22 (18.9)	35.79 (9.0)	—	397.77 (100.0)
5.	Delhi	306.9 (31.9)	278.2 (28.9)	19.9 (2.1)	202.9 (21.1)	154.3 (16.0)	—	962.2 (100.0)
6.	Gauhati	85.09 (26.7)	90.72 (28.5)	54.09 (17.0)	60.14 (18.9)	16.06 (5.2)	11.79 (3.7)	317.89 (100.0)
7.	HS Gaur	69.03 (26.4)	48.78 (18.6)	27.20 (10.4)	96.18 (36.7)	20.70 (7.9)	—	261.89 (100.0)
8.	JNU	99.54 (22.0)	60.30 (13.3)	193.96 (42.9)	2.99 (0.7)	43.94 (9.7)	51.49 (11.4)	452.22 (100.0)

(Contd.)

TABLE 2.25 (*Contd.*)

1	2	3	4	5	6	7	8	9
9.	Kerala	260.15 (34.7)	121.56 (16.2)	28.28 (3.8)	306.88 (40.9)	32.65 (4.4)	—	749.52 (100.0)
10.	Kurukshetra	230.89 (44.5)	94.08 (18.1)	61.93 (11.9)	92.59 (17.8)	39.50 (7.7)	—	518.99 (100.0)
11.	Madras	182.40 (25.0)	277.84 (38.1)	20.92 (2.9)	226.09 (31.0)	22.03 (3.0)	—	729.28 (100.0)
12.	Mysore	136.41 (29.4)	130.33 (28.0)	29.49 (6.3)	127.78 (27.5)	40.76 (8.8)	—	464.70 (100.0)
13.	Panjab	287.66 (35.0)	199.48 (24.3)	53.41 (6.5)	141.92 (17.3)	94.05 (11.4)	45.01 (5.5)	821.53 (100.0)
14.	Utkal	158.1 (45.7)	32.2 (9.3)	10.47 (3.0)	135.08 (39.0)	10.40 (3.0)	—	346.25 (100.0)
15.	Visva Bharati	122.6 (35.6)	80.9 (23.5)	36.7 (10.7)	14.97 (4.3)	26.41 (7.7)	62.65 (18.2)	344.23 (100.0)
	Average	182.93 (26.5)	163.49 (23.7)	67.05 (9.7)	117.15 (17.0)	44.69 (6.5)	115.24 (16.7)	690.55 (100.0)

Note : Figures within the parenthesis are the percentages to total.

average, 26.5 per cent was incurred on administration, the minimum being 13.7 per cent for Annamalai and maximum being 45.7 per cent for Utkal (Table 2.25 col. 3).

The expenditure on common services accounts for, on an average, 23.7 per cent of the total central expenditure for the sample of 15 universities. It may be observed that while the universities like Annamalai, BHU, Gauhati and Madras incurred more expenditure on this category than on administration. The universities like Utkal (9.3 per cent) and JNU (13.3 per cent) spent much less than others on various items under common services.

The expenditure on student services widely varies between 2 to 45 per cent of the total central expenditure, the average for the sample being 9.7 per cent. The major portion of the expenditure on student services was spent, by most universities, on providing scholarships and other extra-curricular activities.

The conduct of examinations is an important activity of the affiliating universities. On an average, it constitutes 17 per cent of the total central expenditure for the year of analysis. It ranged between 3 to 41 per cent of total central expenditure. While there are university to university differences, a relatively higher share of the total expenditure on conduct of examination is spent by the affiliating universities which manage large number of regular and external students. It may be mentioned in passing that whereas Central universities generally incure losses on account of the conduct of examination, most affiliating universities are able to generate surpluses to finance general programmes of universities.[9]

The expenditure on library services varied between 2.3 to 16 per cent of total central expenditure during the period of study. Some of the universities where the expenditure on maintenance of library emerged above the average are University of Delhi (16 per cent), Panjab (11 per cent), JNU (10 per cent) and Calcutta (9 per cent). At the lower end are Annamalai (2.3 per cent), Gauhati (5.2 per cent) and Madras (3.0 per cent).

Some of the universities have their own institutes which are managed and financed by them. Whereas BHU incurred as high as 31 per cent of the total central expenditure, Annamalai spent minimum 3 per cent in 1988-89.

In brief, the composition of expenditure and the pattern of distribution of resources across various functional heads varies a great deal. The allocation of funds for various purposes, in absolute as well as relative terms provide useful information about the thrust areas of university activity. Such data however, hardly lend desirable perspective about the efficiency in use of funds or its adequacy as guaged from the level of expenditure obtaining in other universities which are pursuing comparable programmes and objectives. An attempt is therefore made in the following Chapter 3, to examine the extent of variations across the universities, mainly in terms of per student institutional costs, which is considered as a measure of efficiency in use of funds.

Notes and References

1. *Challenge of Education* (p. 3. 40), Government of India, 1985.
2. See author's Education: An Exercise in Shadow Boxing", *Financial Express,* August 1, 1996.
3. *Education and Economic Development* by the author, AIU, 1987.
4. For a detailed information on university system, see *UGC's Annual Reports and AIU's Handbook.*
5. For comprehensive discussion on the aspects of higher education and employment see *Graduate Unemployment in India* by Azad, J.L., AIU, 1991.
6. This part of the discussion is largely based on Author's *Fiscal Policy for University Development, op.cit.*
7. For a detailed discussion on costs and finance aspects of correspondence courses, see author's *Economics of Distance Higher Education,* Concept, 1992.
8. See *Fiscal Policy...., op.cit.* (Ch. 3).
9. *Ibid., op.cit.* (Ch. 4).

THREE

UNIT COSTS ANALYSIS
Comparison of Per Student Costs of Higher Education

In the preceding Chapter 2, an attempt was made to identify *inter alia* the sources of income of universities and to describe the methods of resource allocation by the funding agencies as well as patterns of distribution of funds among a cross-section of unversities for various programmes. The analysis of results provide desirable perspective on the efforts being made by the funding agencies as well as recipient universities for promoting various programmes of higher education and research in each of the institution. The relevant comparisions reveal the degree of emphasis laid by each institution in promoting higher education in specific areas. The broad trends in distribution of funds across the teaching and research schemes by different universities do not indicate the areas and extent to which certain programmes are under or over funded as judged from either the accpeted normative criteria or the positive levels of allocations as obtaining, to the average extent, among a cross-section of institutions. It may be reiterated that for the purposes of sound planning and effective management of resources, an idea of the degree of efficiency in use of resources is of crucial significance with a view to making appropriate policy intervention to realize the given objectives. Such an important decision is obviously based on a set of efficiency indicators, of which unit costs analysis mainly in terms of per student costs are most valuable ones.

The concept of unit costs denotes the amount of recurrent expenditure spent per student in a given year. The unit costs are calculated either for the educational system as a whole or preferably for certain levels of education, or even for particular institutions or for a particular programme of study. The unit costs indicate the costs of educating one student for one year at the level of the chosen disaggregation. With the help of unit costs, it is possible to make all sorts of comparisions; from one year to the next; from one institution to another and so on. In brief, as a summary statistics, unit costs reveal vital aspects of educational finances pertaining particularly to efficiency in use of resources. However, the unit costs analysis itself indicates very little of interest. It is only when the relevant comparisons are made that it become useful for planning and policy making purposes. Since the unit costs are used primarily for comparisons, it is, therefore, important to exercise great deal of care in computing unit costs. In view of the significance of unit costs analysis, an attempt has been made in this Chapter to estimate per student institutional costs. At the outset, the methodology of estimating per student costs of higher education is described below.

3.1 Approach of Unit Costs Analysis

This study, it may be reiterated, is confined to institutional costs incurred by the select 15 universities during the year 1988-89; for which the latest actual data are available. The institutional costs refers to the recurring and non-recurring expenditure which is financed by the Government grant and the collection of other charges, as already discussed in the previous Chapter. The private costs incurred by students for purchase of books, stationary, transport and other maintenance expenses are not analysed in this study. Likewise, opportunity costs or the benefits foregone due to attending universities are also not discussed. As the higher education institutions are largely financed by the Government, the cost analysis (per student) has been attempted to obtain an idea about efficiency in utilization of resources by different universities.

To this end in view, two sets of unit costs (per student) have been worked out; one is obtained by dividing the total expenditure under each respective category (cost head) by the total enrolment attributable to that category; the other is obtained by dividing the total expenditure by the weighted enrolment, which may be explained as follows.

In order to ensure comparability of results within departments of an institution and across the institutions, it is deemed necessary to make suitable adjustments in the enrolment data pertaining to different courses and levels for the following facts.

First, the costs of teaching of various types and levels of programmes under each discipline naturally varies due to the specific requirements of academic and non-academic staff and other supporting facilities involved in imparting knowledge. For instance, the expenditure on courses related to science and technology education vis-a-vis arts and social sciences differ a great deal due to the use of nature of technology for effective students' learning.

Second, the differences in per student costs are even more pronounced at the successively higher levels of education. As may be expected, the costs of education of a diploma/certificate programme are obviously much less than the costs of doctoral students in every discipline due to the relative duration of course and educational efforts in terms of physical and financial inputs that are required to be made at each successive levels.

Third, the variations in costs occur not merely because of the above factors but also because of the differences in the agencies of the Central and the State Governments which adopt different approaches of funding the universities under their jurisdiction, as already discussed in Chapter 2.

In brief, in order to enhance the contributions of universities to scholastic attainments of students at each successive level of education, the corresponding efforts (or inputs) that are required to be made to impart knowledge of high order should be appropriately reflected in the computation of unit costs. This however, requires the disaggregated data to show the extent of change in financial inputs due to the 'value added' in knowledge at each successive level of graduation in different disciplines. Unfortunately, the requisite data are neither compiled to reflect such dimensions as above nor there is any ingeneous technique which, by making use of existing budgetary data, can be helpful for working out reliable unit costs that can duly indicate relative weights of relevant components of costs. In order to overcome this problem, a set of weights have been evolved with a view to standardizing enrolments in different programmes and making the costs comparable across the institution (Table 3.1). It may be noted that these weights are, in a sense, subjective and are evolved on the basis of our judgement based on normative and positive considerations about relationship between the nature and types of courses and costs, which are generally influenced by such factors as the duration of course programme, infrastructure, such as, lab, equipment and library facilities that are required for promoting teaching and learning process at higher levels in different areas of

TABLE 3.1: Weights Assigned to Different Levels of Education for Computing Equivalent Enrolment

S. No.	Level of Education	Arts/ Commerce	Science/ Agriculture	Engineering/ Medicine
1	2	3	4	5
1.	Under-Graduate	1.0	1.5	2.0
2.	Post-Graduate	1.7	2.25	2.5
3.	Research			
	(1) M.Phil	2.2	3.0	3.0
	(2) Ph.D.	2.8	3.5	3.5
4.	Diploma	0.5	0.5	0.5
5.	Certificate	0.25	0.25	0.25

specialization.

In our attempt to estimate equivalent enrolment centring at undergraduate (UG) level, we have judged from our own crude assessment of the expenditure pattern that the costs of UG (Science) and technical courses are higher by at least, 50 and 100 per cent, respectively, as compared to the UG (Arts) due to relative capital intensity arising from the requirements for infrastructure facilities for effective learning in the fields of science and technology. The probable costs. at the successively higher levels e.g. postgraduate, M.Phil, and Ph.D. under each category should therefore be higher by more or less in the ratios reflected from the weights which have been escalated on the basis of duration of courses and deployment of superior or costly nature of resources as inputs. In order to ensure comparability of the outcome of our exercises, such a manupulation of data was considered necessary because the desirable break up of financial inputs data particularly about the total hours of effective teaching, the average level of payment of salaries of staff associated with teaching and research process in a department, the extent of spill-over costs due to inter-departmental services and sharing of facilities, etc., are not compiled or available. Therefore, no idea is gained from aggregative data about the attributable costs of various programmes. The appropriate weights are therefore helpful to convert enrolment in equivalent terms which allow for computing per student costs of undergraduate level of education in Arts which has been assigned unity as weight. The weights for other levels of education have been scaled up or down, as explained and shown in above Table 3.1. The results of unit costs, thus, reflect as to what may be the approximate costs differences in various programmes rather than what it is when unweighted or absolute level of enrolment for an institution is used. In order to minimise distortions owing to the system of assigning weights for standardizing enrolments, unit costs have also been computed separately for different faculties and departments.

An obvious advantage of showing unit costs at undergraduate level (Arts) is to indicate a somewhat realistic and acceptable level of costs of education for other colleges and universities which are not covered in this study. The per student costs of different levels and types of education are worked out by using the above weights which allow for the standardization of the costs at undergraduate levels of education for all the universities in the sample with a view to ensuring comparability among them. The application of these weights have essentially minimised the variations in costs of different types and levels of programmes. The estimated unit costs, thus, reveal the degree of efficiency in use of resources as compared to the average level of costs obtaining for all the universities.

The per student costs by faculty and by major disciplines have also been estimated and presented separately for the weighted (per student equivalent) and unweighted (per student non-equivalent) enrolment. The relevant break-up of the payment of salaries of teaching and non-teaching staff as well as the expenses on account of non-salary items incurred by each of the faculty/department are also estimated by employing the method discussed above. The Central expenditure attributable to each faculty/department has also been estimated on *pro rata* basis and shown separately for each faculty/department. Inspite of the inherent limitations of this method of attributable expenditure for each faculty/department, the maintenance of budgetary records currently in practice by the universities hardly allow for arriving at realistic costs. Therefore, the expenditure on central administration and common services have been appropriated in the ratio of the faculty/departmental expenditure to the total expenditure.

3.2 The Results

The plan of presentation of the results of unit costs exercises is as under. At the outset, per student costs estimated on the basis of full time equivalent students i.e. by applying weighted enrolment are displayed on comparative basis for all the universities in the sample. Subsequently, faculty and departmentwise unit costs are demonstrated. The major faculties for which computation of unit costs have been made are Faculties of Arts, Science, Commerce and Law. Likewise, the major subject areas that have been chosen for cost analysis are: Economics, Education, English, Hindi, History, Library Science, Music, Political Science, Psychology, Sanskrit, Sociology, Botany, Chemistry, Computer Science, Geography, Geology, Mathematics, Physics, Statistics, Zoology and Anthropology. These are the major departments which are commonly run by the universities in the sample. Some departments may be major ones in certain universities but we have examined only those departments which exist in other universities as well.

3.2.1 Institutional Unit Costs

Before we proceed further, it would be appropriate to briefly discuss macro-level results for all the institutions of higher education in the country. As against the average unit costs for the country as a whole, the corresponding figure for the sample of universities can be compared to gain an idea of the extent of closeness or divergence of individual universities from the national average.

Table 3.2 shows per student expenditure for different types of institutions of higher education for the period 1971-72 to 1983-84 (latest). The growth of per student costs at 1970-71 prices indicate a rising trend for the category of institutions, namely, universities, institutions of national importance, research institutions and the colleges of general and professional education. Over the period of thirteen years, i.e. 1971 to 1983, the per student costs have increased by about 270 and 46 per cent, respectively, at current and constant prices. The relative growth rates for other types of institutions may also be seen in Table 3.2.

The pattern of distribution of expenditure across the major heads of expenditure, namely, payment of salaries to teaching and non-teaching staff, maintenance of building, equipment, library, games and sports, etc., are shown in Table 3.3, which shows for the year 1983-84, the national average level of allocation of financial resources, in absolute as well as relative terms, with respect to the major categories of institutions of higher education. For universities,

TABLE 3.2: Per Student Recurring Expenditure by Types of Institutions of Higher Education—All India (1971-72 to 1983-84)

(in Rs.)

Years	Universities*	Institutions of National Education	Research Institutions	Colleges for General Education	Colleges for Professional
1971-72	3050 (2905)	12266 (11682)	11795 (11233)	408 (389)	1550 (1476)
1972-73	3311 (2830)	14566 (12450)	12649 (10811)	422 (361)	1621 (1385)
1973-74@	3589 (2582)	15263 (10981)	17717 (12746)	449 (323)	1717 (1235)
1974-75	3866 (2386)	15972 (9859)	20079 (12394)	492 (304)	1857 (1146)
1975-76	4123 (2660)	18309 (11812)	12817 (8269)	552 (356)	2063 (1331)
1976-77	4595 (2768)	21638 (13035)	30106 (18136)	692 (417)	1787 (1077)
1977-78	4757 (2766)	20661 (12012)	20895 (12148)	706 (410)	1988 (1156)
1978-79	6196 (3520)	22582 (12831)	25343 (14399)	782 (444)	2021 (1148)
1979-80	7143 (3536)	22416 (11097)	26639 (13188)	931 (411)	2180 (1079)

(Contd.)

TABLE 3.2 *(Contd.)*

Years	Universities*	Institutions of National Education	Research Institutions	Colleges for General Education	Colleges for Professional
1980-81	9600 (4286)	25500 (11384)	24600 (10982)	996 (445)	2543 (1135)
1981-82	10100 (4040)	30800 (12320)	21700 (8680)	1098 (439)	2773 (1109)
1982-83	11200 (4226)	38900 (14679)	30200 (11396)	999 (377)	3859 (1456)
1983-84	11253 (4246)	44423 (16763)	42209 (15928)	1068 (403)	4245 (1602)

Note:*Excluding Institutions Deemed to be Universities.

@ Figures were estimated through Interpolation method as published data for the year were not available.

Note : Figures within parenthesis indicate values at Constant (1970-71) prices. These were calculated with the help of GNP deflators.

Source: Calculated on the basis of data available in the various issues of Education in India, Ministry of Human Resource Development, Government of India, New Delhi.

TABLE 3.3: Composition of Recurring Expenditure (Per Student) by Institutions, 1983-84—All India

(in Rs.)

S.No.	University	Salaries & Allowances of Teaching Staff	Salaries & Allowances of Non-Teaching Staff	Maintenance of buildings	Maintenance of equipment & furniture	Apparatus chemicals & consumable stores	Libraries	Stipends, scholarships & other Financial concessions	Games & Sports	Hostel	Other Items	Total Recurring cost	Total Recurring cost for 1988-89*
1	2	3	4	5	6	7	8	9	10	11	12	13	14
1.	Universities	3573 (31.7)	2765 (24.6)	331 (2.9)	149 (1.3)	469 (4.2)	243 (2.2)	385 (3.4)	49 (0.4)	169 (1.5)	3120 (27.8)	11253 (100.0)	18121
2.	Deemed to be Universities	6495 (33.9)	3880 (20.2)	683 (3.6)	119 (0.6)	1401 (7.3)	344 (1.8)	991 (5.2)	38 (0.2)	129 (0.7)	5092 (26.5)	19170 (100.0)	30873
3.	Institutions of National Importance	12623 (28.4)	8237 (18.5)	3423 (7.7)	2622 (5.9)	5684 (12.8)	527 (1.2)	2445 (5.5)	206 (0.5)	476 (1.1)	8180 (18.4)	44423 (100.0)	71965
4.	Res. Institutions	14420 (34.2)	10797 (25.6)	696 (1.6)	501 (1.2)	3240 (7.7)	857 (2.0)	819 (1.9)	3 (0.01)	2 (0.01)	10874 (25.8)	42209 (100.0)	68379
5.	Colleges (Degree standard & above)	828 (56.3)	311 (21.2)	21 (1.4)	15 (1.0)	44 (3.0)	25 (1.7)	91 (6.2)	10 (0.7)	13 (0.9)	112 (7.6)	1470 (100.0)	2381

(Contd.)

TABLE 3.3 *(Contd.)*

1	2	3	4	5	6	7	8	9	10	11	12	13	14
6.	College (Below degree standard)	1100 (56.0)	384 (19.6)	34 (1.7)	55 (2.8)	59 (3.0)	12 (0.6)	141 (7.2)	7 (0.3)	14 (0.8)	157 (8.0)	1963 (100.0)	3180

* Projected figures on the basis of 1983-84 figures.

Note : Figures within parenthesis are the percentages to the total.

Source: Computed from the Education in India, Part-I and Part-II, 1983-84, Ministry of Human Resource Development, Department of Education, Govt. of India, New Delhi.

it shows that per student costs emerged a little over eleven thousand, in 1983-84, which in 1988-89 i.e. the base year for this study, comes to eighteen thousand, when the 1983-84 figure is projected at the rate of 10 per cent per annum which is the approximate rate of increase in prices in the country during the period.

Of the total expenditure, 56.3 per cent was spent on the payment of salaries of teaching (31.7 per cent) and non-teaching staff (24.6 per cent). Some of the essential teaching-learning support services like maintenance of equipment and furniture (1.13 per cent) apparatus, chemical and consumable items (4.2 per cent) and libraries (2.2 per cent) together accounted for marely 7.7 per cent of the total expenditure. The miscellaneous items alone accounted for as high as 27.8 per cent. Higher magnitudes of expenditure on miscellaneous items (27.8 per cent) and payment of salaries to non-teaching staff (24.6 per cent) indicates excessive allocation for non-academic activities. These results based on simple national average must be born in mind while assessing the appropriateness of our exercises for a cross-section of universities, the estimates of which are presented below.

Table 3.4 demonstrates per student costs computed on the basis of weighted enrolment. It indicates the break up of expenditure with respect to major categories, namely, recurring and non-recurring expenditure. The operating costs, i.e. recurring expenditure, is further divided into departmental and central costs; wherein the items of expenditure for such items as the payment of salaries to the staff and non-salary expenses are separately shown. The following observations may be made:

(i) the average non-recurring expenditure comes to about 10 per cent of the total expenditure for the 15 universities; the remaining 90 per cent is accounted for by the recurring expenditure;

(ii) the highest share of 51 per cent is accounted for by the central costs which obviously hide wide variations across the universities. While the central costs are as high as 74 and 71 per cent for the Universities of Kerala and Kurukshetra, respectively, the corresponding shares for the Universities of Annamalai and Banaras are 32 and 40 per cent, respectively;

(iii) the proportion of salary and non-salary expenses in the total central costs are almost equal i.e. 26 and 25 per cent respectively;

TABLE 3.4: Institutional Costs-Per Student Equivalent (PSE) by Major Components, 1988-89

(in Rs.)

Sl. No.	Components of Cost	Recurring-Cost							Non-Recurring	Grand Total
		Departmental Cost				Central Cost				
		Salary & Allowances				Salary & Allowances				
	Universities	Teaching Staff	Non-Teaching Staff	Non-Salary Items	Total	Non-Teaching Staff	Non-Salary Items	Total	Cost	
1	2	3	4	5	6 = (3+4+5)	7	8	9 = (7+8)	10	11 = (6+9+10)
1.	Annamalai	1490 (19.7)	4406 (5.9)	811 (10.7)	2747 (36.3)	549 (7.3)	1834 (24.3)	2383 (31.6)	2426 (32.1)	7556 (100.0)
2.	BHU	7625 (26.2)	4762 (16.4)	1405 (4.8)	13792 (47.4)	5471 (18.8)	6294 (21.6)	11765 (40.4)	3545 (12.2)	29102 (100.0)
3.	Bombay	1272 (11.6)	1427 (13.1)	835 (7.7)	3534 (32.4)	3421 (31.3)	2767 (25.3)	6188 (56.6)	1198 (11.0)	10920 (100.0)
4.	Calcutta	8692 (36.1)	3752 (15.6)	1759 (7.3)	14203 (59.0)	8787 (36.5)	693 (2.9)	9480 (39.4)	366 (1.5)	24049 (100.0)
5.	Delhi	2089 (26.4)	1023 (12.9)	387 (4.9)	3499 (44.2)	2166 (27.4)	1972 (24.9)	4138 (52.3)	281 (3.5)	7918 (100.0)
6.	Gauhati	1616 (21.8)	515 (6.9)	158 (2.1)	2289 (30.8)	3266 (44.0)	1576 (21.3)	4842 (65.3)	288 (3.9)	7419 (100.0)

(Contd.)

TABLE 3.4 (*Contd.*)

1	2	3	4	5	6 = (3+4+5)	7	8	9 = (7+8)	10	11 = (6+9+10)
7.	HS Gaur	1031	697	369	2097	1168	1623	2791	319	5207
		(19.8)	(13.4)	(7.1)	(40.3)	(22.4)	(31.2)	(53.6)	(6.1)	(100.0)
8.	JNU	3726	492	1084	5302	3484	8396	11880	3796	20978
		(17.8)	(2.3)	(5.2)	(25.3)	(16.6)	(40.0)	(56.6)	(18.1)	(100.0)
9.	Kerala	2445	984	484	3913	8715	7158	15873	1598	21384
		(11.4)	(4.6)	(2.3)	(18.3)	(40.7)	(33.5)	(74.2)	(7.5)	(100.0)
10.	Kurukshetra	3648	1143	449	5240	7664	5971	13635	268	19143
		(19.1)	(6.0)	(2.3)	(27.4)	(40.0)	(31.2)	(71.2)	(1.4)	(100.0)
11.	Madras	2633	1305	868	4806	3179	8902	12081	2983	19870
		(13.2)	(6.6)	(4.4)	(24.2)	(16.0)	(44.8)	(60.8)	(15.0)	(100.0)
12.	Mysore	2700	980	180	3860	2912	2828	5740	3242	12842
		(21.0)	(7.6)	(1.4)	(30.0)	(22.7)	(22.0)	(44.7)	(25.2)	(100.0)
13.	Panjab	4720	2014	2598	9332	5260	2988	8248	971	18551
		(25.4)	(10.9)	(14.0)	(50.3)	(28.3)	(16.1)	(44.4)	(5.2)	(100.0)
14.	Utkal	1250	599	185	2034	1902	2100	4002	596	6632
		(18.8)	(9.0)	(2.8)	(30.6)	(28.7)	(37.7)	(60.4)	(9.0)	(100.0)
15.	Visva Bharati	6145	1673	724	8542	8451	3330	11781	118	20441
		(30.1)	(8.2)	(3.5)	(41.8)	(41.3)	(16.3)	(57.6)	(0.6)	(100.0)
	Average	3199	1502	805	5506	3700	3466	7166	1429	14101
		(22.66)	(10.64)	(5.70)	(39.00)	(26.21)	(24.55)	(50.76)	(10.24)	(100.0)

(*Contd.*)

TABLE 3.4 *(Contd.)*

1	2	3	4	5	6 = (3+4+5)	7	8	9 = (7+8)	10	11 = (6+9+10)
	Average*	2550 (20.93)	1011 (8.30)	737 (6.05)	4298 (35.28)	3259 (26.75)	3270 (26.84)	6529 (53.59)	1356 (11.13)	12183 (100.0)
	CV (%)	73.6	85.2	82.2	70.3	63.4	69.1	52.0	92.58	48.49

* Excluding the too high and too low cases namely the Universities of Banaras, Calcutta and HS Gaur.

Note : Figures within parenthesis are the percentages to total.

(iv) the share of academic departments in the total expenditure comes to 39 per cent, of which 23 and 11 per cent, respectively, is accounted for by the payment of salaries of teaching and non-teaching staff and the remaining share about 6 per cent is spent on non-salary items within the departments;

(v) the average per student costs for the sample universities has emerge marginally above Rs. 14,000, which after eliminating too high and too low cases comes to about Rs. 12,000 per year; and

(vi) there are glaring variations in unit costs; the highest being Rs. 29,000 for BHU and the lowest of Rs. 5200 for HS Gaur. Lastly, the co-efficient of variations indicate wide differences in the total unit costs and its components across the universities.

Table 3.5 reveals the per student costs which have been estimated by using un-weighted or absolute enrolment. It may be observed that the difference between per student equivalent and non-equivalent (PSE and PSNE) is vary wide and the latter is higher than former by 66 per cent. The break-up of components of per student costs of each university can be seen in the aforementioned Table 3.5. At this point of time, an important observation which can be made is that as against the national average costs (per student) in 1988-89, of Rs. 18,000 as already shown in Table 3.3., the corresponding average figure for the sample universities comes to Rs. 23,000. The estimate of PSE costs which largely nullifies the factors contributing for variations in costs, comes to Rs. 14,000 per year.

3.2.2 Per Student Costs by Faculties

An attempt was also made to decompose the total institutional costs by the major faculties, namely arts, sciences, commerce and law. The unit costs based on equivalent enrolment are shown in Tables 3.6 through 3.9. The need for analysing unit costs by faculties arises from the fact that the salient features of academic faculties associated with the nature of activities carried out by them do not get properly reflected in the total institutional costs due mainly to gross aggregation of data. It becomes therefore necessary to isolate the costs that can be ascribed to the type and level of programmes offered by different faculties. Such dis-aggregated data prove to be useful for drawing relevant inferences about allocation of resources

TABLE 3.5: Institutional Costs—Per Student Non-Equivalent (PSNE) by Major Components, 1988-89

(in Rs.)

Sl. No.	Components of Cost	Recurring-Cost							Non-Recurring	Grand Total	Difference between PSNE Cost to PSE cost per unit
		Departmental Cost				Central Cost					
		Salary & Allowances				Salary & Allowances					
	Universities	Teaching Staff	Non-Teaching Staff	Non-Salary Items	Total	Non-Teaching Staff	Non-Salary Items	Total			
1	2	3	4	5	6 = (3+4+5)	7	8	9 = (7+8)	10	11 = (6+9+10)	12
1.	Annamalai	2978 (20.0)	691 (4.6)	1621 (10.9)	5290 (35.5)	1096 (7.3)	3667 (24.6)	4763 (31.9)	4050 (32.5)	14903 (100.0)	7347
2.	BHU	7625 (26.2)	4762 (16.4)	1405 (4.8)	13791 (47.4)	5471 (18.5)	6294 (21.6)	11765 (40.4)	3545 (12.2)	29102 (100.0)	—
3.	Bombay	2385 (11.6)	2677 (13.1)	1567 (7.6)	6629 (32.3)	6416 (31.3)	5189 (25.3)	11605 (56.7)	2247 (11.0)	20481 (100.0)	9561
4.	Calcutta	8692 (36.1)	3752 (15.6)	1759 (7.3)	14203 (59.0)	8787 (36.5)	693 (2.9)	9480 (39.4)	366 (1.5)	24049 (100.0)	—
5.	Delhi	3377 (26.4)	1654 (12.9)	626 (4.9)	5657 (44.2)	3503 (27.3)	3190 (24.9)	6693 (52.3)	454 (3.5)	12804 (100.0)	4886
6.	Gauhati	3169 (23.5)	1010 (7.5)	310 (2.3)	4489 (33.3)	5669 (42.1)	2735 (20.3)	8404 (62.4)	563 (4.2)	13456 (100.0)	6037
7.	HS Gaur	1674 (19.8)	1131 (13.4)	598 (7.1)	3403 (40.3)	1896 (22.4)	2634 (31.2)	4530 (53.6)	517 (6.1)	8450 (100.0)	3243

(Contd.)

TABLE 3.5 *(Contd.)*

1	2	3	4	5	6 = (3+4+5)	7	8	9 = (7+8)	10	11 = (6+9+10)	12
8.	JNU	6973 (19.7)	920 (2.6)	2029 (5.7)	9922 (28.0)	6522 (18.4)	15711 (44.4)	22233 (62.8)	3260 (9.2)	35415 (100.0)	14437
9.	Kerala	5624 (11.4)	2263 (4.6)	1114 (2.3)	9001 (18.1)	20045 (47.7)	16464 (33.5)	36509 (74.2)	3675 (7.5)	49185 (100.0)	27801
10.	Kurukshetra	6940 (20.2)	2174 (6.3)	853 (2.6)	9967 (29.1)	13378 (39.0)	10423 (30.4)	23801 (69.4)	513 (1.5)	34281 (100.0)	15138
11.	Madras	5422 (13.2)	2688 (6.6)	1788 (4.4)	9898 (24.2)	6549 (16.0)	48333 (44.8)	24882 (60.8)	6142 (15.0)	40922 (100.0)	21052
12.	Mysore	4950 (24.8)	1793 (9.1)	330 (1.6)	7073 (35.5)	4167 (20.9)	4046 (20.3)	8213 (41.2)	4640 (23.3)	19928 (100.0)	7086
13.	Panjab	8552 (25.4)	3650 (10.8)	4708 (14.0)	16910 (50.3)	9531 (20.3)	5414 (16.1)	14945 (44.4)	1759 (5.3)	33614 (100.0)	15063
14.	Utkal	2418 (18.8)	1160 (9.0)	357 (2.8)	3935 (30.7)	3680 (28.7)	4064 (31.7)	7744 (60.4)	1152 (9.0)	12831 (100.0)	6199
15.	Visva Bharati	7965 (30.1)	2168 (8.2)	938 (3.5)	11071 (41.8)	10953 (41.3)	4316 (16.3)	15269 (57.6)	153 (0.6)	26493 (100.0)	6052
	Average	5376 (22.9)	2525 (10.8)	1353 (5.8)	9254 (39.5)	6217 (26.5)	5825 (24.8)	12042 (51.3)	2168 (9.2)	23464 (100.0)	9363 (66.4)
	CV (%)	47	54	82	46	68	81	65	87	47	

Note : Figures within parenthesis are the percentages to the total.

TABLE 3.6: Recurrent Cost Per Student Equivalent 1988-89
(Faculty of Arts)

(in Rs.)

S. No.	Universities	Departmental Cost				Central Cost	Grand Total
		Salaries & Teaching Staff	Allowances of Non-Teaching Staff	Non-Salary Items	Total		
1	2	3	4	5	6 = (3+4+5)	7	8 = (6+7)
1.	Annamalai	2756 (47.8)	234 (4.0)	90 (1.6)	3080 (53.4)	2688 (46.6)	5768 (100.0)
2.	BHU*	3562 (39.8)	926 (10.3)	129 (1.9)	4617 (51.6)	4324 (48.4)	8941 (100.0)
3.	Bombay	946 (19.4)	612 (12.6)	212 (4.3)	1771 (36.3)	3100 (63.7)	4871 (100.0)
4.	Calcutta*	4862 (54.4)	1496 (16.7)	256 (2.9)	6616 (74.0)	2321 (26.0)	8935 (100.0)
5.	Delhi	2439 (30.8)	876 (11.0)	317 (4.0)	3632 (45.8)	4297 (54.2)	7929 (100.0)
6.	Gauhati	1499 (29.5)	242 (4.7)	32 (0.6)	1773 (34.8)	3319 (65.2)	5092 (100.0)

(Contd.)

TABLE 3.6 *(Contd.)*

1	2	3	4	5	6 = (3+4+5)	7	8 = (6+7)
7.	HS Gaur	1518 (28.1)	666 (12.3)	127 (2.3)	2311 (42.8)	3084 (57.2)	5395 (100.0)
8.	JNU	3569 (25.0)	429 (3.0)	334 (2.3)	4332 (30.3)	9963 (69.7)	14295 (100.0)
9.	Kerala	2463 (13.6)	946 (5.2)	165 (0.9)	3574 (19.7)	14493 (80.3)	18067 (100.0)
10.	Kurukshetra	3868 (20.8)	962 (5.2)	664 (3.6)	5494 (29.6)	13118 (70.4)	18612 (100.0)
11.	Madras	2848 (19.0)	982 (6.5)	435 (2.9)	4265 (28.4)	10736 (71.6)	15001 (100.0)
12.	Mysore	2642 (31.9)	772 (9.3)	81 (1.0)	3495 (42.2)	4776 (57.8)	8271 (100.0)
13.	Panjab	4360 (35.8)	1395 (11.5)	981 (8.1)	6736 (55.4)	5427 (44.6)	12163 (100.0)
14.	Utkal	1740 (25.3)	432 (16.3)	148 (2.1)	2320 (33.7)	4564 (66.3)	6884 (100.0)
15.	Visva Bharati	5494 (31.15)	778 (4.41)	252 (1.43)	6524 (36.39)	11112 (63.01)	17636 (100.0)
	Average	3007 (29.43)	797 (7.80)	287 (2.81)	4091 (40.04)	6126 (59.96)	10217 (100.0)

(Contd.)

TABLE 3.6 *(Contd.)*

1	2	3	4	5	6 = (3+4+5)	7	8 = (6+7)
	Average**	2893 (31.71)	782 (8.57)	280 (3.07)	3955 (43.35)	5168 (56.65)	9123 (100.0)
	CV (%)	44	47	89	42	64	48

* Since the relevant break-up of enrolments was not available, the unit cost are worked out using un-weighted enrolment data.

** Excluding too-high cost figures, namely the Universities of Kerala and Kurukshetra.

Note : Figures within parenthesis are the percentages to respective total.

at the faculty levels. Hence, this attempt. The following major conclusions emerge from faculty-wise analysis of unit costs.

Table 3.6 reveals for the faculty of arts that:

(i) The per student costs of higher education falls in the range of about Rs. 5 to 18 thousand per year, the average, for 15 universities, being Rs. 10,000. Of this, 60 per cent constitutes central costs. The payment of salaries to teachers comes to Rs. 3,000 per student which account for about 30 per cent of the total costs at the faculty level;

(ii) The unit costs of education under the faculty of science (Table 3.7) has emerged almost twice the costs of arts faculty. The range of costs varies from the lowest of about 4,000 for Annamalai to the highest of Rs. 35,000 for Calcutta; the average being marginally above Rs. 18,000. Although the per student payment of salaries of teachers has emerged lower for science faculty, as compared to arts, the percentage share is merely 22 per cent since the signficant proportion of expenses is captured by the salary of supporting staff and non-salary items in science faculty.

(iii) The per student costs of commerce and management (Table 3.8) comes to about 7,000 and the average per student payment of salaries to teachers comes to Rs. 2,100 which is much lower as compared to the corresponding figures for the faculties of arts and science.

(iv) The costs of the faculty of law (Table 3.9) are the lowest at Rs. 2,500 per student per year. The unit costs however vary from the lowest figure of about Rs. 800 for HS Gaur to Rs. 11,000 for BHU.

(v) In all the above four faculties, inter-university differences, as explained by the co-efficient of variations are extremely wide with respect to almost every item of expenditure, the causes of which would be explored later.

(vi) The academic (departmental) costs for all the faculties fall in the range of 40 to 45 per cent while the remaining share is accounted for by the central costs.

(vii) As regards the professional education, the per student costs of the faculty of agriculture has emerged Rs. one lakh. Almost fifty per cent of the total costs was accounted for by non-academic activities;

TABLE 3.7: Recurrent Cost Per Student Equivalent 1988-89
(Faculty of Science)

(in Rs.)

S. No.	Universities	Departmental Cost: Salaries and Allowances of: Teaching Staff	Departmental Cost: Salaries and Allowances of: Non-Teaching Staff	Departmental Cost: Non-Salary Items	Departmental Cost: Total	Central Cost	Grand Total
1	2	3	4	5	6 = (3+4+5)	7	8 = (6+7)
1.	Annamalai	1744 (40.7)	402 (9.4)	140 (3.3)	2286 (53.4)	1994 (46.6)	4280 (100.0)
2.	BHU	7836 (31.3)	4482 (17.9)	1672 (6.7)	13990 (55.9)	11058 (44.1)	25048 (100.0)
3.	Bombay	1980 (11.6)	2565 (15.0)	1651 (9.7)	6196 (36.3)	10850 (63.7)	17046 (100.0)
4.	Calcutta	16691 (47.5)	9686 (27.6)	3674 (10.4)	30051 (85.5)	5083 (14.5)	35134 (100.0)
5.	Delhi	3461 (23.0)	2427 (16.2)	997 (6.6)	6885 (45.8)	8147 (54.2)	15032 (100.0)
6.	Gauhati	2847 (21.8)	1265 (9.7)	437 (3.4)	4549 (34.9)	8487 (65.1)	13036 (100.0)

(Contd.)

TABLE 3.7 *(Contd.)*

1	2	3	4	5	6 = (3+4+5)	7	8 = (6+7)
7.	HS Gaur	1031 (20.5)	697 (13.8)	244 (4.8)	1972 (39.1)	3071 (60.9)	5043 (100.0)
8.	JNU	4824 (14.5)	783 (2.4)	4718 (14.2)	10325 (31.1)	22909 (68.9)	33234 (100.0)
9.	Kerala	2666 (11.1)	1134 (4.7)	971 (4.0)	4771 (19.8)	19352 (80.2)	24123 (100.0)
10.	Kurukshetra	4925 (19.9)	1891 (7.7)	476 (1.9)	7292 (29.5)	17403 (70.5)	24695 (100.0)
11.	Madras	3257 (13.6)	1944 (8.1)	1630 (6.8)	6831 (28.5)	17167 (71.5)	23998 (100.0)
12.	Mysore	2819 (26.2)	1383 (12.8)	344 (3.2)	4546 (42.2)	6213 (57.8)	10759 (100.0)
13.	Panjab	6879 (28.2)	3696 (15.2)	2462 (10.1)	13037 (53.5)	11330 (46.5)	24367 (100.0)
14.	Utkal	3707 (19.1)	2167 (11.2)	671 (3.4)	6545 (33.7)	12878 (66.3)	19423 (100.0)
15.	Visva Bharati	3951 (27.7)	981 (6.9)	1052 (7.4)	5984 (42.0)	8280 (58.0)	14264 (100.0)
	Average	4056 (22.06)	2253 (12.26)	1671 (9.09)	7980 (43.41)	10402 (56.59)	18382 (100.0)

(Contd.)

TABLE 3.7 *(Contd.)*

1	2	3	4	5	6 = (3+4+5)	7	8 = (6+7)
	Average*	4270 (20.26)	2630 (12.48)	1882 (8.93)	8782 (41.67)	12288 (58.33)	21070 (100.0)
	CV (%)	83	98	93	83	56	47

* Excluding too-high cost figures i.e. Annamalai, Calcutta, HS Gaur, JNU.

Note : Figures within parenthesis are the percentages to respective total.

TABLE 3.8: Recurrent Cost Per Student Equivalent 1988-89
(Faculty of Commerce and Management)

(in Rs.)

S. No.	Universities	Departmental Cost				Central Cost	Grand Total
		Salaries & Allowances of		Non-Salary Items	Total		
		Teaching Staff	Non-Teaching Staff				
1	2	3	4	5	6 = (3+4+5)	7	8 = (6+7)
1.	Annamalai	757 (49.1)	20 (1.9)	40 (2.6)	826 (53.6)	714 (46.4)	1540 (100.0)
2.	BHU*	4024 (53.3)	178 (2.3)	18 (0.3)	4220 (55.9)	3328 (44.1)	7548 (100.0)
3.	Bombay	1622 (18.2)	532 (6.0)	1075 (12.1)	3229 (36.3)	5656 (63.7)	8885 (100.0)
4.	Calcutta	1447 (73.4)	187 (9.5)	111 (5.6)	1745 (88.5)	227 (11.5)	1972 (100.0)
5.	Delhi	1821 (32.4)	50 (10.7)	2572 (2.7)	3042 (45.8)	2572 (54.2)	5614 (100.0)
6.	Gauhati	696 (20.1)	400 (11.6)	103 (3.0)	1199 (34.7)	2256 (65.3)	3455 (100.0)
7.	HS Gaur	695 (28.0)	316 (12.7)	49 (2.0)	1060 (42.7)	1418 (57.3)	2478 (100.0)

(Contd.)

TABLE 3.8 *(Contd.)*

1	2	3	4	5	6 = (3+4+5)	7	8 = (6+7)
8.	Kerala	958 (13.6)	383 (5.4)	53 (0.8)	1394 (19.8)	5656 (80.2)	7050 (100.0)
9.	Kurukshetra	4470 (22.6)	1105 (5.6)	256 (1.3)	5831 (29.5)	13944 (70.5)	19775 (100.0)
10.	Madras	828 (19.7)	305 (7.3)	52 (1.2)	1184 (28.2)	3017 (71.8)	4201 (100.0)
11.	Mysore	1787 (35.9)	272 (5.5)	26 (0.5)	2085 (41.9)	2894 (58.1)	4979 (100.0)
12.	Panjab	4671 (39.0)	1171 (9.8)	594 (5.0)	6436 (53.8)	5530 (46.2)	11966 (100.0)
13.	Utkal	1972 (23.1)	531 (6.3)	369 (4.3)	2872 (33.7)	5652 (66.3)	8524 (100.0)
	Average	2121 (31.87)	610 (9.17)	273 (4.10)	3004 (45.14)	3650 (54.86)	6654 (100.0)
	Average*	2144 (29.56)	714 (9.84)	316 (4.36)	3174 (43.76)	4078 (56.24)	7252 (100.0)
	CV (%)	73	73	137	68	85	73

* Computed after excluding the too high and too low figures i.e. in Universities of Annamalai, Calcutta, Kurukshetra and Panjab.

Note : Figures within parenthesis are the percentages to respective total.

TABLE 3.9: Recurrent Cost Per Student Equivalent 1988-89
(Faculty of Law)

(in Rs.)

S. No.	Universities	Departmental Cost				Central Cost	Grand Total
		Salaries & Allowances of		Non-Salary Items	Total		
		Teaching Staff	Non-Teaching Staff				
1	2	3	4	5	6 = (3+4+5)	7	8 = (6+7)
1.	BHU	5813 (53.7)	—	142 (1.3)	5955 (55.0)	4871 (45.0)	10826 (100.0)
2.	Bombay	340 (18.9)	281 (15.6)	49 (2.3)	663 (36.8)	1134 (63.2)	1797 (100.0)
3.	Calcutta	1118 (69.9)	—	400 (25.0)	1518 (94.9)	81 (5.1)	1599 (100.0)
4.	Delhi	893 (32.1)	352 (12.6)	31 (1.1)	1276 (45.8)	1510 (54.2)	2786 (100.0)
5.	Gauhati	425 (28.1)	54 (3.6)	50 (3.3)	529 (35.0)	982 (65.0)	1511 (100.0)
6.	HS Gaur	191 (24.1)	123 (15.5)	26 (3.3)	340 (42.9)	453 (57.1)	793 (100.0)
7.	Kerala	238 (5.5)	99 (2.5)	447 (11.2)	784 (19.6)	3212 (80.4)	3996 (100.0)

(Contd.)

TABLE 3.9 (*Contd.*)

1	2	3	4	5	6 = (3+4+5)	7	8 = (6+7)
8.	Kurukshetra	1016 (21.0)	396 (8.2)	19 (0.4)	1421 (29.6)	3404 (70.4)	4835 (100.0)
9.	Madras	1458 (22.4)	398 (6.1)	28 (0.4)	1885 (28.9)	4620 (71.1)	6505 (100.0)
10.	Mysore	4981 (53.6)	660 (7.1)	283 (3.0)	5924 (63.8)	3363 (36.2)	9287 (100.0)
11.	Panjab	1275 (39.3)	359 (11.1)	79 (2.4)	1713 (52.8)	1530 (47.2)	3243 (100.0)
12.	Utkal	274 (17.2)	244 (13.3)	50 (3.2)	535 (33.7)	1053 (66.3)	1588 (100.0)
	Average	797 (30.8)	318 (12.3)	60 (2.3)	1121 (43.4)	1463 (56.6)	2584 (100.0)
	Average*	704 (26.3)	280 (11.2)	59 (2.4)	1043 (41.9)	1445 (58.1)	2488 (100.0)
	CV (%)	125	62	116	104	75	80

* Computed after excluding too high and too low figures i.e. in Universities of Banaras Hindu, HS Gaur and Mysore.
Note : Figures within the parenthesis are the percentages to respective totals.

(viii) The per student costs of the faculty of engineering and technology was Rs. 1.27 lakhs.

(ix) The unit costs for the faculty of medicine with respect to the select universities was about Rs. 1.5 lakhs.

3.2.3 Per Student Costs by Disciplines

We may now proceed to examine the unit costs at a somewhat more disaggregative level i.e. by major disciplines. Table 3.10 and 3.11 display per student costs of major subjects in arts, social science and natural sciences. The break-ups of unit costs in terms of salary and non-salary components are shown separately elsewhere. As before, both the types of estimates i.e. in terms of per student equivalent and non-equivalent are presented with a view to gaining an idea about the magnitude of institutional costs as obtaining in different universities. Inter-university and intra-departments variations in costs, it may be noted are extremely glaring, a phenomena observed at all levels of analysis as discussed before. The estimate of per student costs for different subjects in various universities may be seen in the Table 3.10 which reveal *inter alia* the following with respect to the sample:

(i) The average per student costs (equ.) of teaching Economics is estimated to be over Rs. 8,000 of which 64 per cent is attributable to central costs. The corresponding costs (non-equ.) is over Rs. 16,000. The CV is estimated to be 57 per cent. Of the total departmental costs, on an average, 70 and 25 per cent were spent as wage of teaching staff and teaching supporting staff, respectively. Teaching material account only 5 per cent for the Economics discipline.

(ii) The costs (equ.) of teaching History, about Rs, 14,000 has surprisingly emerged higher than the costs of economics but the inter-university differences as indicated by CV of 131 per cent are very wide. The central costs is nearly 37 per cent. The average departmental cost of history was Rs. 3,607 per annum of which 78 and 18 per cent was incurred on salary of teaching and non-teaching staff and remaining 4 per cent on non-salary expenses mainly teaching materials.

(iii) The per student costs (equ. and non-equ.) of Political Science are estimated to be nearly Rs. 7,000 and Rs. 13,000

TABLE 3.10: Discipline-wise Unit Costs (PSE and PSNE)
(Faculty of Arts and Social Sciences)

(in Rs.)

S. No.	University	Economics		History		Pol. Science		Sociology		Anthropology		Lib. Science	
1	2	3		4		5		6		7		8	
		PSE	PSNE	PSE	PSNE	PSE	PSNE	PSE	PSNE	PSE	PSNE	PSE	PSNE
1.	Annamalai	5463	9748	7301	11473	8950	15566	4496	7767	—	—	4266	3792
		(3554)	(6341)	(4776)	(7506)	(5850)	(10174)	(2925)	(5052)	—	—	(672)	(597)
2.	Bombay	5832	11547	4291	7870	5212	9567	5286	9764	—	—	6030	6113
		(3702)	(7332)	(2728)	(5001)	(3308)	(6089)	(3348)	(6184)	—	—	(3309)	(4491)
3.	Calcutta	—	19286	—	16795	—	10194	—	15435	—	—	—	8962
		—	(10894)	—	(10682)	—	(6475)	—	(9776)	—	—	—	(5414)
4.	Delhi	10717	20809	8044	17775	3720	8100	12820	26655	9487	30633	8636	8551
		(5798)	(11327)	(4340)	(9591)	(2024)	(4407)	(6956)	(14462)	(5155)	(16643)	(4668)	(4626)
5.	Gauhati	4647	8356	4774	8433	2394	4493	—	—	28042	73531	15477	16292
		(3493)	(6281)	(3559)	(6286)	(1784)	(3349)	—	—	(20771)	(54467)	(11567)	(12175)
6.	HS Gaur	1642	1899	2444	17800	5353	9725	11170	20611	4926	8265	6995	9865
		(1131)	(1331)	(1677)	(9839)	(3556)	(6844)	(6967)	(14390)	(2949)	(4948)	(4233)	(5970)
7.	Kerala	6676	15021	10173	20709	10144	20285	17184	21858	—	—	10185	20742
		(4356)	(9801)	(6678)	(13594)	(6608)	(13216)	(31641)	(14347)	—	—	(6681)	(13619)
8.	Kurukshetra	8195	14672	10516	18884	8948	16079	8043	14544	—	—	6821	9752
		(4097)	(7336)	(5258)	(9449)	(4469)	(8044)	(4022)	(7277)	—	—	(3407)	(4879)

(Contd.)

TABLE 3.10 *(Contd.)*

1	2	3		4		5		6		7		8	
9.	Madras	19449 (13945)	39211 (28115)	22423 (12527)	46495 (25496)	10647 (7628)	17466 (12514)	5735 (4033)	11080 (7985)	— —	— —	30145 (21551)	56632 (40516)
10.	Mysore	13223 (9312)	23452 (16519)	11707 (8273)	22877 (16110)	6806 (4793)	11767 (8287)	22616 (20399)	38866 (34970)	— —	— —	12890 (9077)	18769 (13217)
11.	Panjab	8795 (4069)	24141 (15872)	67686 (3771)	23052 (15160)	6976 (3229)	21503 (14140)	11516 (5325)	33436 (21985)	18630 (8661)	58099 (38062)	8869 (4103)	19772 (13000)
12.	Utkal	7394 (5510)	12770 (9517)	5880 (4377)	10106 (7524)	4564 (3399)	7833 (5834)	24373 (18143)	43990 (32746)	19636 (14680)	46119 (34476)	9235 (6154)	18478 (13846)
	Average	8367 (5361)	16743 (10889)	14113 (5269)	18522 (11353)	6701 (4241)	12715 (8281)	12324 (8586)	54000 (15379)	16144 (10443)	43329 (29719)	10868 (6856)	16478 (11029)
	Average*	7882 (4877)	15980 (10122)	8979 (4862)	16790 (10574)	6741 (4137)	12658 (8188)	11796 (7817)	21361 (14350)	15917 (9499)	44950 (29727)	9460 (5911)	13732 (9124)
	CV (%)	57 (65)	57 (63)	131 (57)	56 (49)	41 (43)	42 (42)	57 (75)	207 (67)	56 (69)	58 (65)	65 (83)	84 (94)
	CV (%)*	35 (38)	35 (36)	68 (35)	31 (32)	33 (35)	34 (36)	50 (68)	47 (59)	35 (51)	31 (39)	32 (48)	40 (47)

TABLE 3.10 *(Contd.)*

S. No.	University	English		Hindi		Sanskrit		Psychology		Music		Education	
1	2	3		4		5		6		7		8	
		PSE	PSNE	PSE	PSNE	PSE	PSNE	PSE	PSNE	PSE	PSNE	PSE	PSNE
1.	Annamalai	18854 (12109)	29907 (19518)	14143 (9214)	9900 (6450)	77000 (51000)	51333 (34000)	20095 (13128)	34073 (22261)	— —	7594 (4946)	3343 (2179)	4387 (2860)
2.	Bombay	2769 (1759)	5215 (3319)	1563 (991)	2853 (1809)	11058 (7061)	15666 (10003)	4432 (2821)	8531 (5429)	4418 (2811)	7851 (4995)	4178 (2638)	8354 (5276)
3.	Calcutta	— —	8790 (5536)	— —	11964 (7709)	— —	59006 (55671)	— —	97458 (58466)	— —	63030 (38853)	— —	6222 (3563)
4.	Delhi	10385 (5620)	21408 (11586)	7507 (4079)	15740 (8552)	3170 (1721)	1898 (1012)	9892 (5382)	23163 (12600)	12242 (6642)	29079 (15774)	15899 (8596)	29579 (15992)
5.	Gauhati	4580 (3435)	8607 (6455)	15314 (11369)	29276 (21735)	29545 (22123)	52025 (38957)	14511 (10569)	26428 (19250)	— —	— —	5030 (3678)	9047 (6615)
6.	HS Gaur	17396 (12248)	30987 (21816)	28496 (20041)	50540 (35546)	18258 (12810)	26816 (18815)	38876 (23576)	71423 (49771)	18235 (12785)	18236 (12785)	— —	— —
7.	Kerala	9964 (6539)	18491 (12098)	— —	— —	3590 (880)	9687 (2375)	13750 (8993)	28874 (18885)	— —	— —	8927 (5847)	20485 (13418)
8.	Kurukshetra	6463 (3233)	10880 (5433)	4698 (2352)	9532 (4769)	14878 (7428)	28050 (14031)	11670 (5693)	21611 (10798)	7734 (3862)	16885 (8438)	26202 (13102)	46491 (2346)
9.	Madras	5300 (3789)	10238 (7321)	13650 (9815)	26209 (18845)	17662 (12640)	36206 (25911)	15543 (11101)	32983 (23556)	22806 (16302)	42368 (30286)	15694 (11217)	29958 (21414)

(Contd.)

TABLE 3.10 *(Contd.)*

1	2	3		4		5		6		7		8	
10.	Mysore	7864 (5538)	10792 (7600)	16627 (11672)	32773 (23079)	9150 (6443)	18577 (13082)	20240 (16725)	21922 (15477)	— —	— —	15542 (10944)	27143 (19114)
11.	Utkal	15465 (11529)	26292 (19600)	— —	— —	8725 (6496)	15130 (11287)	17592 (13107)	30906 (23026)	— —	— —	— —	— —
	Average	9522 (6221)	16510 (10926)	11675 (7880)	19740 (13416)	18378 (12074)	28393 (20204)	15982 (10486)	35423 (23145)	12581 (7842)	27010 (17063)	12369 (7315)	22359 (13906)
	Average*	9397 (6048)	16193 (10598)	10716 (7128)	18001 (12101)	13554 (8899)	27981 (18577)	14721 (9884)	31908 (21385)	12065 (6985)	24242 (15451)	11682 (7222)	21589 (13580)
	CV (%)	57 (63)	54 (57)	72 (79)	74 (81)	113 (118)	63 (79)	56 (58)	69 (67)	54 (69)	70 (72)	61 (55)	68 (64)
	CV (%)*	52 (58)	47 (50)	51 (61)	55 (64)	56 (70)	52 (60)	28 (42)	46 (51)	37 (58)	51 (59)	47 (46)	59 (56)

U : Not computed due to non-availability of disaggregated data.
PSE : Per Student Equivalent.
PSNE : Per Student Non-Equivalent.
Note : The figures in parenthesis are the total central costs per student.
* : Computed after the eleminating too high and too low figures.

respectively, of which central costs comprise 63 per cent. The remaining 27 per cent cost per student are departmental cost incurred on salary and allowance of teaching and teaching supporting (non-teaching) staff and non-salary items. More than 3/4th portion of departmental cost was spent on wages of teaching staff.

(iv) The costs (equ.) of teaching Sociology is almost double the costs of Political Science. In some universities, the reported data pertaining to the actual enrolment and level of expenditure are of highly suspect; and therefore, much reliance cannot be placed in per student costs (non-equ.) of Sociology;

(v) The costs of Anthropology are similarly higher about Rs. 16 thousand (equ.). Ninty-four per cent of the total departmental costs was spent on salary and allowances of teaching and non-teaching staff and remaining only 6 per cent accounted for non-salary expenses in the department.

(vi) The costs of Library Science has emerged about eleven (equ.) and sixteen thousand, (non-equ.) of which central costs being 63 per cent. The departmental cost per student for the sample universities was estimated about Rs. 4,000 per annum of which 74, 16 and 19 per cent account for salary to teaching staff, non-teaching staff and non-salary items, respectively.

(vii) The costs per student (equ.) of teaching Psychology and Education are estimated to be Rs. 16 and 12 thousand respectively. The average departmental cost for Psychology and Education was Rs. 8,287 and Rs. 4,814 respectively, of which more 90 per cent was incurred on salary account.

(viii) Teaching of major languages namely, English, Hindi and Sanskrit surprisingly involves even much more expenditure than social sciences subjects. For instance, per student (equ.) costs of teaching the above languages for the sample of universities are worked out to be as high as ten, twelve and eighteen thousands respectively for English, Hindi and Sanskrit. Of the total departmental cost in the above language departments, about 96 to 98 per cent expenses were incurred on wages of teaching and non-teaching staff. This is despite the fact that most universities rely on class room teaching, as in social sciences, and they hardly use educational technology like audio-visual equipment for teaching of the above languages. The central costs are generally over 60 per cent of the total units costs.

(ix) The per student (equ.) costs of teaching Botany and Zoology have come out to be about Rs. 15,000 and Rs, 17,000, respectively, for the sample, the unit costs, per student (non-equ.) are very close for both the subjects, over Rs. 15,000. Inter-university differences are quite wide (Table 3.11). The departmental cost is also very close as both the disciplines accounted for between Rs. 6,000 to 7,000. The salary for teaching and non-teaching staff was estimated at Rs. 5,000 to 6,000. The non-salary expenses incurred by both the departments were between Rs. 7,000 to 12,000 of the total departmental cost per unit per annum.

(x) The per student (equ.) costs of teaching of Physics and Chemistry were Rs. 15,000 and Rs. 20,000 respectively, the corresponding figures for per student (non-equ.) costs have emerged as high as rupees 54 and 66 thousand (Table 3.11). The central costs are about 60 per cent of the total unit costs in both the departments. The average departmental costs per student accounted for Rs. 7815 for Chemistry and Rs. 5502 for Physics of which 75 and 92 per cent were spent on salary of teaching and non-teaching staff and remaining share accounted for maintaining of labs and other expenses.

(xi) As compared to other science subjects, discussed above the per student (equ.) costs of teaching Statistics and Mathematics are the lowest at about Rs. eleven and twelve or (non-equ.) costs are about Rs. 36,000 and Rs. 31,000, of which 66 and 74 per cent are attributable to central cost, respectively. The salary component emerged to be 92 to 97 per cent of the total departmental cost which is justified because both are the non-lab based courses.

Finally, while the unit costs of both types i.e. per student (equ. and non-equ.) are generally higher, as expected, for science subjects than social sciences, the differences within the specific groups of disciplines or institutions mainly in terms of the level of allocation of funds, as compared to the average extent, are very wide. As the central costs have generally emerged over 60 per cent, it is important to analyse them in greater detail in the following section.

TABLE 3.11: Discipline-wise Unit Cost (PSE and PSNE)
(Faculty of Science)

(in Rs.)

S. No.	University	Botany		Chemistry		Mathematics		Physics		Statistics		Zoology	
1	2	3		4		5		6		7		8	
		PSE	PSNE	PSE	PSNE	PSE	PSNE	PSE	PSNE	PSE	PSNE	PSE	PSNE
1.	Annamalai	5773 (3764)	13818 (8945)	7207 (4698)	17140 (11173)	5308 (3461)	12626 (8233)	5774 (3762)	13762 (8967)	6688 (4355)	15494 (10089)	4054 (2644)	9467 (6174)
2.	Bombay	— —	— —	15759 (10011)	41800 (26555)	7190 (4577)	17276 (10997)	11716 (7457)	29244 (18581)	5734 (3694)	14030 (9040)	— —	— —
3.	Calcutta	— —	142081 (88160)	— —	117333 (78632)	— —	53025 (35138)	— —	86857 (53935)	— —	89341 (55833)	— —	86691 (54435)
4.	Delhi	22632 (12327)	76669 (41549)	17011 (9216)	57811 (31321)	7568 (4103)	24442 (13252)	10889 (5892)	38113 (20622)	11536 (6281)	36291 (19779)	33464 (18249)	109576 (59309).
5.	Gauhati	16595 (12272)	40632 (30046)	26881 (19846)	66353 (48987)	6216 (4610)	14831 (11000)	20688 (15318)	52913 (39177)	23313 (17287)	48699 (36111)	14210 (10522)	36105 (26735)
6.	HS Gaur	4602 (2752)	7913 (4732)	18493 (11052)	52645 (31462)	3798 (2278)	9905 (5939)	3087 (1830)	4796 (2868)	— —	— —	3698 (2211)	6165 (3686)
7.	Kerala	30445 (17744)	82601 (54016)	12620 (8257)	40702 (26630)	7314 (4775)	18755 (12244)	9384 (6149)	26951 (17659)	10423 (5219)	47397 (31119)	— —	— —

(Contd.)

TABLE 3.11 *(Contd.)*

1	2	3		4		5		6		7		8	
8.	Kurukshetra	15834 (7922)	38743 (19385)	20731 (10363)	51932 (25960)	6943 (3475)	15889 (7953)	17571 (8779)	43610 (21789)	9217 (6580)	23381 (1702)	21637 (10826)	53852 (26945)
9.	Madras	8887 (1804)	30010 (6092)	24322 (17419)	59037 (42244)	42701 (30571)	94891 (67936)	14026 (10045)	37472 (26837)	10630 (15091)	23589 (16840)	6325 (1238)	18227 (3567)
10.	Mysore	9484 (6681)	25852 (18212)	17052 (12012)	41254 (29060)	11729 (8249)	28506 (20047)	16298 (11481)	39422 (27771)	5151 (2397)	36889 (25985)	12708 (8952)	33503 (23600)
11.	Panjab	12086 (5614)	48765 (31946)	36004 (16742)	178440 (116880)	13981 (6507)	44437 (29108)	26365 (12260)	93017 (60927)	16129 (12058)	32085 (21011)	39173 (18217)	119561 (78319)
12.	Utkal	25293 (18918)	58239 (43560)	26786 (17304)	75384 (56414)	16111 (12061)	35601 (26652)	30505 (22813)	67214 (50266)	16128 (12058)	35481 (26527)	21547 (16109)	47135 (35239)
	Average	15163 (8980)	51383 (31513)	20262 (12447)	66652 (43776)	11714 (7697)	30848 (20710)	15118 (9617)	54445 (30529)	11495 (8502)	36607 (29970)	17424 (9885)	52028 (31801)
	Average*	14573 (8516)	46136 (28194)	19964 (12486)	60425 (39726)	9151 (5757)	26539 (17466)	14746 (9015)	43552 (28560)	10811 (8675)	33256 (22129)	16278 (9787)	49319 (29500)
	CV (%)	57 (67)	74 (79)	39 (38)	64 (66)	93 (104)	78 (85)	55 (61)	60 (67)	49 (61)	57 (48)	73 (68)	78 (80)

(Contd.)

TABLE 3.11 *(Contd.)*

1	2	3		4		5		6		7		8	
	CV (%)*	47 (62)	50 (58)	25 (29)	38 (43)	42 (49)	52 (55)	42 (40)	48 (51)	35 (57)	33 (39)	62 (64)	69 (68)

U: Indicate not computed due to non-availability of disaggregated data.

* Computed after the eliminating too high and too low figures.

Note : The figures in parenthesis are central cost per student.

PSE.: Per Student Equivalent

PSNE: Per Student Non-Equivalent

3.2.4 Central Costs

Thus far, we have examined the unit costs (per student) at the institutional and faculty levels. The costs of major disciplines of studies have also been examined to demonstrate the extent of divergence in allocation of funds for specific areas of study among the universities. The attributable shares of central costs in each case have also been indicated. As the costs of central administration and common services have invariably emerged more than sixty per cent in most universities, it would be worth while to scrutinize the major constituents of the central costs. As already described before, the major components of central costs, which we have identified are as under:

(i) General administration which includes expenditure on staff engaged by the offices of Vice-Chancellor, Pro-Vice-Chancellor, Registrar, Finance, etc. The expenses on account of payment of salaries to staff and other non-pay items, incurred by these offices are included in this category.

(ii) Common services include such expenses on salary and non-salary items as maintenance of building, roads, garden, water and electricity supply, health centres and other related expenses of these departments.

(iii) Expenditure on student services includes such items as games and sports, hostel facilities, recreational and cultural activities, students' union, National Cadet Corps (NCC), students study centres, scouts and moutaineering and other expenses related to students' welfare and related activities.

(iv) Expenditure on library facilities include payment of salary to library staff, the expenses incurred on purchase of newspapers and magazines and maintenance of books, journals and equipments which facilities the use of library.

(v) For the conduct of examinations especially in affiliating university expenditure is incurred. The expenses relating to payment of salary of staff engaged in conduct of examination, remuneration to examiners, printing of question papers, printing and preparation of answer books, computer charges, travelling allowances of examiners and moderators, stationary and other related expenses are included under separate category i.e. examinations.

(vi) The expenses on institutions maintained by some universities are shown separately. The institutions in this category are generally schools under the management of universities.

Against this backdrop, the results of unit costs analysis with respect to non-teaching units of universities are presented in Table 3.12. The following observations may be made:

First, on an average, Rs. 8552 per student was spent during the year under reference, of which 53 per cent was on account of payment of salaries of the staff and the remaining share was incurred on non-pay items of expenditure. Inter-University differences are glaring so much so that Annamalai spent as low as Rs. 549 per student on salaries of non-teaching units whereas the corresponding costs for Calcutta, Kerala were more than Rs. 8700. The differences across the universities are even more pronounced with respect to non-salary expenditure.

Second, of the various components of non-teaching units, the expenditure on central administration was a major chunk (35 per cent), of which a major share has been on, as usual, for payment of salaries, about 22 per cent.

Third, the unit costs of common services emerged as to the second largest, i.e. 28 per cent and, as before, inter-university differences under the respective sub-heads are wide.

Fourth, the expenses on examination accounted for 19 per cent, a major share of over 12 per cent was spent on non-salary items. In absolute terms, per student costs of conducting examination has emerged more than Rs. 1620 per year. The disparities across the universities are very glaring not only among the unitary and affiliating universities but also within the respective groups. For instance, in affiliating universities, namely Kerala and Madras per student costs of conducting examination have emerged as high as Rs. 6500 and Rs. 3745 per year respectively, the corresponding figure for Calcutta (Rs. 1793) and Gauhati (Rs. 916) are obviously too low. Likewise, per student costs for central universities namely, Banaras, Delhi and Visva Bharati also varies even when the enrolment data relating to different types and levels of educational programmes were duly standardized to make them comparable.

It is important to mention that when suitable adjustment in enrolment data attributable to affiliated colleges was made and accordingly expenditure data were adjusted on *pro rata* basis so as to

TABLE 3.12: Recurrent Expenditure Per Student on Central Services (PSE), 1988-89

(in Rs.)

S.No.	Universities	Administration			Common Services			Examination			Library			Student Serv.			Univ. Main Inst.			Total		
		S	NS	T	S	NS	T	S	NS	T	S	NS	T	S	NS	T	S	NS	T	S	NS	T
1.	Annamalai	163	166	329	135	325	459	48	365	413	34	22	56	166	913	1079	3	44	47	549	1834	2383
		6.8	7.0	13.8	5.7	13.6	19.3	2.0	15.3	17.3	1.4	0.9	2.3	7.0	38.3	45.3	0.1	1.8	1.9	23.0	77.0	100.0
2.	BHU	1822	2311	4133	2290	2655	4945	164	642	806	334	10	344	861	676	1537	—	—	—	5471	6294	11765
		15.5	19.6	35.1	19.5	22.5	42.0	1.4	5.4	6.8	2.8	0.1	2.9	7.3	5.7	13.0				46.5	53.5	100.0
3.	Bombay	1830	309	2139	1061	955	2016	193	1002	1195	246	174	420	141	276	417	—	—	—	3421	2766	6187
		29.6	5.0	34.6	17.1	15.4	32.5	3.1	16.2	19.3	4.0	2.8	6.8	2.3	4.5	6.8				55.3	44.7	100.0
4.	Calcutta	3157	—	3157	2243	249	2492	1793	—	1793	688	166	854	906	279	1185	—	—	—	8787	693	9481
		33.3		33.3	23.6	2.6	26.2	18.9		18.9	7.2	1.7	9.0	9.5	2.9	12.5				92.7	7.3	100.0
5.	Delhi	891	429	1320	411	202	613	209	664	873	422	241	663	52	34	86	181	402	583	2166	1972	4138
		21.5	10.4	31.9	9.9	4.9	14.8	5.0	16.0	21.0	10.2	5.8	16.0	1.2	0.8	2.0	4.4	9.7	14.1	52.3	47.7	100.0
6.	Gauhati	950	346	1296	879	501	1380	288	628	916	234	11	245	739	85	824	176	3	179	3266	1574	4840
		19.6	7.1	26.7	18.2	10.3	28.5	5.9	13.0	18.9	4.8	0.2	5.0	15.3	1.7	17.0	3.6	0.10	3.7	67.5	32.5	100.0
7.	HS Gaur	433	214	647	277	515	792	165	737	902	96	98	194	197	58	255	—	—	—	1168	1623	2790
		15.5	7.7	23.2	9.9	18.5	28.4	5.9	26.4	32.3	3.4	3.5	6.9	7.1	2.1	9.2				41.9	38.1	100.0
8.	JNU	1188	2671	3859	1157	2105	3262	—	45	45*	608	655	1263	531	2920	3451	—	—	—	3484	83961	1880
		10.0	22.5	32.5	9.7	17.8	27.5		0.4	0.4	5.1	5.5	10.6	4.5	24.6	29.1				29.3	70.7	100.0
9.	Kerala	2769	2740	5509	1859	713	2574	3245	3254	6499	681	10	691	159	440	599	—	—	—	8715	7157	15873
		17.4	17.3	34.7	11.7	4.5	16.2	20.4	20.5	40.9	4.3	0.1	9.4	1.0	4.8	3.8				54.9	45.1	100.0

(Contd.)

TABLE 3.12 *(Contd.)*

	S	NS	T	S	NS	T	S	NS	T	S	NS	T	S	NS	T	S	NS	T	S	NS	T
10. Kurukshetra	4319	3397	7716	1583	714	2297	376	758	1134	523	445	968	863	657	1520	—	—	—	7664	59711	3635
	31.7	24.9	56.6	11.6	5.2	16.8	2.8	5.6	8.4	3.8	3.3	7.1	6.3	4.8	11.1				56.2	43.8	100.0
12. Madras	1551	1471	3022	89	4513	4602	1147	2598	3745	354	11	365	38	309	347	—	—	—	3179	8902	12081
	19.5	9.8	29.3	18.1	10.0	28.1	5.3	22.2	27.5	4.7	4.0	8.7	3.1	3.2	6.3				50.7	49.3	100.0
13. Panjab	2850	155	3005	1424	660	2084	—	1483	1483	447	536	983	420	138	558	119	16	135	5260	2988	8248
	34.5	1.9	36.4	17.3	8.0	25.3		18.0	18.0	5.4	6.5	11.9	5.1	1.7	6.8	1.4	0.2	1.6	63.8	36.2	100.0
14. Utkal	1104	815	1918	309	48	357	330	1166	1496	108	7	115	50	65	115	—	—	—	1901	2100	4001
	27.5	20.4	47.9	7.7	1.2	8.9	8.2	29.1	37.3	2.7	0.2	2.9	1.2	1.6	2.8				47.5	52.5	100.0
15. Visva Bharati	3194	1005	4199	4024	995	5018	167	312	479	406	447	853	660	571	1231	—	—	—	8450	3330	11780
	27.1	8.5	35.6	34.2	8.4	42.6	1.4	2.6	4.0	3.4	3.8	7.2	5.6	4.8	10.4				71.7	28.3	100.0
Average	1868	1128	2996	1294	1071	2365	574	1046	1620	374	214	588	404	514	918	32	31	63	4543	4009	8552
	21.8	13.3	35.1	15.1	12.5	27.6	6.7	12.2	18.9	4.4	2.5	6.9	4.7	6.0	10.7	0.4	0.4	0.8	53.1	46.9	100.0

Note: S — Salary

NS — Non-Salary items

T — Total (Salary & Non-salary expenses)

(—) — break-up not available/not applicable.

* — The salary component of examination section is included in general administration.

estimate relevant unit costs, the emerging figures were substantially lower for the affiliating universities as indicated below. The average unit costs on account of examination came down to Rs. 250 as against Rs. 1650 for unadjusted data.

Incidently, it may be mentioned that, unit costs of examination for affiliating universities, after netting out the costs attributable to colleges emerged as follows: Bombay (71), Calcutta (50), Delhi (309), Gauhati (89), HS Gaur (121), Kerala (260), Kurukshetra (123), Madras (200), Mysore (323), Panjab (300) and Utkal (324).

Fifth, the unit costs of student services is estimated to be over Rs. 900 per student per year which is about 11 per cent of the total expenditure of non-teaching units. The costs of facilities, other than staff salaries, are marginally higher than the salary component. In terms of relative priority, Annamalai and JNU spent as high as 45 and 29 per cent respectively, of the total expenditure, on non-teaching units. While the absolute cost level of students' services was the highest for JNU (Rs. 3451 per student), most universities spent below the average indicated above.

Sixth, the costs of library facilities were about Rs. 590 per student (7 per cent) which is largely accounted for (4.4 per cent) by the staff salaries while the expenditure on purchase and maintenance of books, journals and equipments, etc., was much less (2.5 per cent).

Lastly, the overall pattern of distribution of costs of administring the university and providing necessary support for academic development revealed considerable dependence on non-academic staff and excessive bureaucratization of universities which have the tendency to spend more on paraphernalia that hardly go into the process of nurturing and improving the quality of educational programmes. Even the non-teaching units like libraries spent more on payment of salaries than purchase of books and other reading materials which are so crucial for improving learning attainments.

3.2.5 Sources of Variations in Unit Costs

The differences in unit costs of higher education are attributable to a number of factors, the most important of them are as under:

First, the input costs of education at all the levels of aggregation, as estimated for this study, have revealed considerable variations across the universities as is evident from coefficient of variations (CVs) discussed above. The universities in India are financed by different agencies of the Centre and the States, namely the University Grants Commission (UGC) and the Department of Education of the State Governments which provide funds on plan and non-plan basis. While the non-plan expenditure i.e. maintenance, which accounts for a major share for all the universities is provided for on the basis of past trend or on deficit basis mainly under the approved items of expenditure, the plan grants are provided on 100 per cent basis to Central and on matching basis to the State universities. Thus, the gross level of funding is crucially dependent on (a) the level of expenditure already attained in the past due to the extent of expansion and diversification of various programmes; and (b) the ability of a university to arrange for matching component to attract maximum plan grants from the UGC as well as to mobilise resources from non-government sources. The allocations of funds by the Government or its agencies are, thus, not linked with the objective criteria of requirements for teaching and research programmes particularly with regard to predetermined quantity and quality of education. The lack of objectively in distribution of resources is also corroborated from the differences in such determinant of expenditure as student-teacher ratios, pcr student expenditure on salary and non-salary items within a particular type of university and the departments across the universities. The evidence reveal that the funding agencies are not employing normative or positive criteria for determining physical and financial resources for different university programmes. Lack of objectively and uniformity in determining eligibility of universities for funding causes inter-university difference in the levels of funding.

Second, even though there is a uniform structure of scale of pay for the teachers of all the universities in the country, there is no uniformity with respect to either student-teacher ratio for each discipline or ratios of senior to junior teachers or other supporting facilities. The recruitment and promotion policies, particularly in relation to the nature, type and level of programme are seemingly *ad hoc* in most universities, which enjoy autonomous status. Such differences cause variations, due to the differences in structure of scale of pay, in per teacher payments of emoluments which consequently influence per student costs of education. There is neither effective academic planning by the universities, as far as quality and quantity of teaching and research activities are concerned nor the funding agencies stipulate for planning and management of resources by using the fiscal tools to streamline the system's functioning in most economical way. Such inadequacies as this in the management of universities cause variations in resource use, apart from generating diseconomies in carrying out various programmes.

Third, the ratios of students (or teachers) to non-teaching staff also varies a great deal among the universities *inter se* and the departments which may be ascribed to many factors including the nature and level of teaching and research activities. For instance, the affiliating universities and those which are running distance education programmes have to maintain a large administrative and secretarial staff. But, even when the influence of such factors are netted out to ensure comparability of results, it was observed that per student expenditure on account of the payment of salaries to non-teaching staff varied across the universities, which is attributable to variations in the scale of pay of non-teaching staff having comparable educational qualifications, experiences and nature of services. The different states which are at varying stages of development, have adopted their own salary structure and procedures of appointment and promotion of such staff. The differences in salary of non-teaching staff naturally affect the total institutional unit costs. The extent to which the differences in the payment of non-teaching staff influence the total costs could be gauged from the relevant comparisons of the unit costs of services rendered by non-academic staff in different universities.

Fourth, the universities vary in the levels as well as nature of teaching and research programmes as already discussed in Chapter 2. The educational activities in the science and technology fields obviously require higher magnitude of expenditure to be incurred for maintenance of equipment, labs, etc., than the levels of expenditure on non-lab based courses. But, the differences in comparable programmes, even when the factors like undergraduate, postgraduate and research study are duly nullified by assigning progressive weights, are attributable to lack of academic planning or judicious deployment of resources on the basis of minimum requirements for facilities. It emerges that even in the science and technical and professional disciplines, the resources are allocated and utilized in unscientific manner, as is evident from discipline-wise costs (per student) of higher education across the universities.

Fifth, the central costs, especially non-pay items of expenditure are associated with the scale of teaching and research activities and the type of university-affiliating and residential. Even when the data was suitably adjusted, as already discussed before, the central costs (per student) reveal a considerable variations among the universities. With respect to all the levels of classification attempted in this study, the comparisions of per student central costs among different types of universities however lend no guidance with regards to the causes of low or high unit costs.

Finally, while some of the causes of variations in unit costs have been identified, it is difficult to indicate or measure the extent to which each factor is responsible in influencing the costs. Insufficient data and lack of a proper methodology to deal with poor quality of data are the main constraints that impinge upon the efforts to undertake such exercises.

FOUR

COST EFFECTIVENESS OF UNIVERSITIES

Analysis of Student's Performance and Unit Costs

The economic evaluation of comparable programmes offered by a large number of institutions is useful for gaining an idea about the efficiency in use of resources which forms the basis for assessing economic viability of educational activities and for ensuring judicious allocation of resources. In this context, the use of the concept of efficiency, which refers to the relationship between input costs and their effects in regard to the outcome of objectives of alternative programmes/institutions, is of immense value for educational planners. While the relative performance of different institutions of education system in making economic use physical and financial resources refers to internal efficiency of the system, the impact of the outcome of educational activities, which encompasses the quality of relevant programmes, on the society and economy refers to external efficiency of the system. The overall assessment of educational performance is usually made by the analysis of cost-effectiveness of programmes/institutions, on comparative basis, which duly takes into account the unit costs and some measure of academic achievements. In the preceding Chapter 3, our discussion was mainly confined to internal effiiciency of higher education system which entail economic use of resources. In this Chapter, an attempt is made to discuss the aspects having significant bearing on the external efficiency of the system. In other words, we seek to examine the students' performance in terms of their learning attainments. Such assessments give an indication of the quality of educated manpower produced by the system to manage and guide the destiny of nation in its efforts to build up an enlightened and prosperous society.

The data limitations, it must be noted, are enormous and do not allow for measuring external efficiency of the university system. Therefore, no attempt has been made to assess the positive or negative impacts of university activities on different socio-economic aspects of the country. But, the evidences relating to the performance of universities, which we seek to discuss herein below, would hopefully lend perspectives on external efficiency of universities. In effect, thus, an idea of cost-effectiveness of universities would be gained to effect policy changes.

The analysis of unit costs in Chapter 3 revealed the level of allocation of resources for comparable programmes and indicated the relative efficiency of universities in utilization of funds under various heads of expenditure. In essence, the results of unit costs analysis provide an idea of the extent of financial inputs (per student) made by different universities on comparable programmes with a view to realizing the common educational objectives pursues by them. Although, it is generally argued that higher the magnitude of financial inputs, given the expected degree of fiscal prudence which ought to be observed by the institutions in management of resources, the higher would be thc quality and quantity of outputs of educated and trained persons. In other words, on the *a priori* the performance of institutions in delivery of educational services is tightly and positively related to level of expenditure, as an indicator of adequacy of facilities for teaching and learning. The question, however, is whether there is enough empirical support for this theoretical expectation? Are the funding agencies and the recipient institutions exercising due care in planning and execution of various educational activities and management of funds to justify the levels of investments that are being made? These questions need to be examined to test the above hypotheses.

In the light of evidence related to financial inputs, already discussed before, and other performance indicators presented in this chapter, we shall explore to answer the above questions. In order to test the reliability of unit costs as an indicator of efficiency in use of funds, it would be worthwhile to examine the effects of the pattern of allocation of resources, as obtaining among different institutions, on the university performance as measured in terms of students' learning attainment i.e. the examination results as well as, the relevant comparisons of students' performance vis-a-vis the indicators like the unit costs and student-teacher (ST) ratios. It is important to note that in making such comparisons, it is assumed that the characteristics of students populations, the tools of assessment of students' achievements at the examinations, etc., are comparable across the universities. Against this backdrop, the results of various exercises carried out by us may be discussed below.

4.1 Macro Level Assessment: All India

To begin with, it would be worthwhile to obtain an idea of the overall performance, of Indian universities, in different levels of courses. The latest examination results at all India level which we could gather, were those pertaining to 1982-83. And, we assume that as far as qualitative improvements in teaching and learning process is concerned there has been no appreciable change since then. The results for the sample universities relating to 1988-89, may, therefore be taken as largely comparable. The unit costs of higher education both at the all India level and for a cross-section of universities as discussed in Chapter 3, and the consequent evidences pertaining to students' performance may lend desirable perspective on cost-effectiveness of higher education. With this end in view, the combined results for all the universities in India are presented in Table 4.1, which demonstrate for the year 1982-83 that:

(i) Of the total number of students who appeared in the final year examinations for various degree level courses, 59.3 passed out and 12.9 per cent students of those who passed scored first division (i.e. 60 per cent and above marks);

(ii) Undergraduate students i.e. BA/B.Sc./B.Com. comprised 64.1 per cent of the total appeared students. Of those who appeared, merely 53.6 per cent passed and merely 10.5 per cent could score first division and above marks;

(iii) The proportion of undergraduate honours i.e. B.A./B.Sc./ B. Com. (Hons) was estimated to be 5 per cent. Of the total number of appeared students, 71.9 per cent passed and the share of students who scored more than 60 per cent marks stood at 13 per cent;

(iv) This proportion of students in M.A./M.Sc./M.Com. together, constituted 13.9 per cent of the total appeared students. Of those who passed (66.7 per cent), merely 13.4 per cent scored

TABLE 4.1: Students' Performance: 1982-83, All India

S. No.	Examination	No. Appeared	No. Passed	I Div.	II Div.	III Div.
1	B.A.	538881 (100.0)	296962 (55.1)	14925 (2.8)	81269 (15.1)	161677 (30.0)
2	B.A. (Hons)	42073 (100.0)	30027 (71.4)	2446 (5.8)	18857 (44.8)	8325 (19.8)
3	M.A.	152847 (100.0)	101954 (66.7)	7762 (5.1)	41242 (27.0)	37371 (24.4)
4	B.Sc.	180357 (100.0)	95001 (52.7)	28564 (15.8)	33255 (18.4)	23584 (13.1)
5	B.Sc. (Hons)	18346 (100.0)	13019 (70.9)	3600 (19.6)	7362 (40.1)	1885 (10.3)
6	B.Sc. Home Sc.	3143 (100.0)	2665 (84.8)	584 (18.6)	1185 (37.7)	189 (6.0)
7	M.Sc.	24009 (100.0)	18675 (77.8)	8328 (34.7)	6831 (28.4)	1301 (5.4)
8	M.Sc. Home Sc.	576 (100.0)	515 (89.4)	213 (37.0)	129 (22.4)	30 (5.2)
9	B. Com.	255879 (100.0)	130887 (51.1)	11373 (4.4)	42212 (16.5)	63802 (24.9)
10	B. Com. (Hons)	16647 (100.0)	12378 (74.3)	1166 (7.0)	6586 (39.6)	4504 (27.1)

(Contd.)

TABLE 4.1 *(Contd.)*

S. No.	Examination	No. Appeared	No. Passed	I Div.	II Div.	III Div.
11	M. Com.	33820 (100.0)	19970 (59.0)	2686 (7.9)	8329 (24.6)	7194 (21.3)
12	M.B.A. BIM M.B.M. etc.	2797 (100.0)	2413 (86.3)	1213 (43.4)	569 (20.3)	65 (2.3)
13	B. Ed.	92881 (100.0)	74283 (80.0)	9951 (10.7)	39479 (42.5)	16936 (18.2)
14	M. Ed.	5759 (100.0)	3959 (68.7)	1142 (19.8)	1463 (25.4)	1136 (19.7)
15	B.E. & B. Tech.	24397 (100.0)	19863 (81.4)	12367 (50.7)	3309 (13.6)	743 (3.0)
16	M.E./M. Tech.	2417 (100.0)	1954 (80.8)	1074 (44.4)	282 (11.7)	204 (8.4)
17	LLB.	76068 (100.0)	41637 (54.7)	2516 (3.3)	26403 (34.7)	8964 (11.8)
18	LLM.	1648 (100.0)	599 (36.3)	30 (1.8)	396 (24.0)	13 (7.9)
19	MBBS	16677 (100.0)	10289 (61.7)	—	—	—
20	M.D.	4334 (100.0)	2323 (53.6)	—	—	—

(Contd.)

TABLE 4.1 *(Contd.)*

S. No.	Examination	No. Appeared	No. Passed	I Div.	II Div.	III Div.
21	M.S.	2260 (100.0)	1310 (58.0)	—	—	—
22	BDS. B. Pharm. etc.	2355 (100.0)	1848 (78.5)	—	—	—
23	MDS, M. Pharm. etc.	669 (100.0)	430 (64.3)	—	—	—
24	BAMS	4625 (100.0)	3322 (71.8)	—	—	—
25	MAMS	179 (100.0)	130 (72.6)	—	—	—
26	B.Sc. AG.	8862 (100.0)	8192 (92.4)	1734 (19.6)	1896 (21.4)	62 (0.7)
27	M. Sc.	2817 (100.0)	2609 (92.6)	713 (25.3)	115 (4.1)	11 (0.4)
28	Others (1)	5379 (100.0)	4536 (84.3)	1226 (22.8)	2212 (41.1)	596 (11.1)

Notes:
(a) Figures within parenthesis are the percentages to the total No. of students appeard in the examination.
(b) (-) Indicate break-up of division-wise results are not available.
(c) Others (1) includes postgraduate result of Lib. Science, Physical Education, Social works, Music, Fine Arts, Journalism, etc.
(d) Difference between No. of passed and the total of I div., II div. & III div. is found in original source of data.

Source: University Development in India: Part II, Examination Results, UGC 1982.

first division marks;

(v) In professional disciplines, namely B.E./B.Tech. and M.B.B.S., the pass-out rates were 81.4 and 61.7 per cent respectively; and

(vi) For the rest of the degree courses, the performance rates varied greatly as may be seen in the table referred to above.

It emerges from the foregoing that:

(a) the overall performance of higher education system is very low which may also be construed to mean that wastages as measured in terms of failures are very high;

(b) the endeavours to promote professional development, as measured by the proportion of students in technical/ vocational disciplines, are much less than desired, especially in the context of modernization of economy; and

(c) the achievements, with respect to 'academic excellence' as denoted by the proportion of students passed out with first division (60 per cent and above) marks, are awfully low.

Finally there is much to be desired in so far as improvements in cost-effectiveness of higher education is concerned. Let us see whether the recent results for a cross section of reputed university corroborate the above findings.

4.2 Faculty-wise Assessment of Performance

Table 4.2 through 4.7 present the examination results by the major faculties for the select universities. The relevant break-ups, namely, the overall pass-out rates and the ratios of students qualifying with different divisions are demonstrated, which reveal both the degree of wastage in terms of failures and the extent of academic excellence as measured by the propotion of students who scored sixty per cent i.e. first division or above marks under each faculty of studies having various levels of programmes, already discussed in Chapter 2.

Table 4.2 shows, for the Faculty of Arts, that pass-out rates differ a great deal from a lower limit of 36.5 per cent for Panjab to the higher of 97.6 per cent for Utkal universities i.e. a difference of 61.1 percentage points. Such a wide difference occurred despite the fact that ST ratio was favourable to Panjab. For instance, there was one

TABLE 4.2: Relationship between Students' Performance, Student-Teacher Ratios and Unit Costs (Faculty of Arts and Social Sciences)

S. No.	University	Ist Div. %	IInd Div %	IIIrd Div %	Total Pass Out %	Ist Div as % of Total Pass Out	STR	Unit Costs (in Rs.)
1	Annamalai	28.7	59.0	3.5	91.2	31.5	9	5768
2	BHU	NA	NA	NA	44.0	NA	18	8941
3	Bombay	16.1	40.9	27.5*	84.5	19.0	30	4871
4	Delhi	16.6	31.8	38.9	88.3	18.8	34	7929
5	Gauhati	1.0	36.6	29.9*	67.5	14.0	11	5092
6	Gaur	12.5	39.9	20.8	73.2	17.1	18	5395
7	Kerala	5.60	14.2	31.8*	51.6	10.9	10	18067
8	Kurukshetra	6.6	31.0	25.5	63.1	10.6	8	18612
9	Madras	5.5	20.9	13.8*	40.2	13.5	7	15001
10	Mysore	4.0	14.4	25.9	44.3	19.1	11	8271
11	Panjab	2.6	9.7	24.2	36.5	17.1	8	12163
12	Utkal	NA	NA	NA	97.6	NA	13	6884

Notes :

1. Student Teacher (ST) Ratios which have been computed by dividing unweighted students number by the total number of teachers to the respective faculty.
2. Per student costs (Equivalent) include both Departmental and Central Costs.

NA — Not Available

* Includes Students' passed without division.

Source: Examination Results have been computed from the Annual Reports 1988-89 of each University.

teacher to teach 8 and 13 students, respectively, in the above universities. Similarly, per student costs difference has emerged in the ratio of 1 to 1.8 for the respective universities, which show that even when the input costs for Panjab was higher than other universities, except Kurukshetra, Kerala and Madras, students' performance was comparatively lower despite the fact that ST ratio was favourably very low. The results for Central universities, namely, Delhi (88 per cent) and Banaras (44 per cent) do not compare favourably as there are considerable differences in pass-out rates as well as other vital indicators of performance, namely, ST ratio and unit costs as may be observed in the aforementioned Table 4.2.

As a measure of excellence in academic pursuits, the proportion of students passed with first division shows the relative level of attainments of different universities. For instance, the universities of Annamalai (31.6 per cent), Delhi (18.8 per cent) and Bombay (19.0 per cent) have emerged with better performance than the universities of Panjab (7.1 per cent), Mysore (9.1 per cent), Kurukshetra (10.6 per cent) and Kerala (10.9 per cent). But these results have been obtained by varying levels of financial and physical inputs as may be compared with the ST ratios and the unit costs.

On the *a priori* grounds it may be argued that ST ratio is negatively but tightly related to unit costs, which may be construed to mean that higher the ratio, lower should be the unit costs. The evidence for a cross-section of universities, however, show that there is no systematic relationship between unit costs, and ST ratios as judged from the criteria of goodness of fit of the regression equations. It could also be argued that a low ST ratio (and the corresponding higher unit costs) would have a positive impact of the total productivity of a university, as measured by students' performance. But, the evidence for most universities do not strongly support this theoretical expectation, as the indicators like unit costs, the ratios of first divisioners and the overall pass-out have not only greatly varied among the universities but showed divergent trends.

For instance, Table 4.3 clearly demonstrate that whereas the universities of Annamalai, Bombay and HS Gaur spent the least i.e. Rs. 6,000, they have emerged with high performance rates, i.e. over 70 per cent pass-outs. Conversely, the universities of Madras and Panjab incurred high costs, yet they emerged with low performance rates i.e. below 50 per cent pass-outs.

In the context of the select universities, it can be deduced that

TABLE 4.3: Relationship Between Unit Costs and Students' Performance (Faculties of Arts and Social Sciences)

Cost Range (in Rs.)	Students' Performance (in %)		
	Low (< 50)	Medium (51-70)	High (71 >)
1	2	3	4
Low (<6000)	—	Gauhati	Annamalai, Bombay, HS Gaur
Medium (6001 to 10000)	BHU, Mysore	—	Delhi, Utkal
High (10000>)	Madras, Panjab	Kerala, Kurukshetra	—

there is no empirical support to generalise that university activities suffer due to 'resource crunch' and that a higher magnitude of funds would necessarily lead to improvements in their performance.

In support of above, some further evidence may be examined. Table 4.4 reveals, for the Faculty of Arts, the relationship between ST ratio and the proportion of students having scored 60 per cent and above marks (an indicator of academic excellence). It may be argued that ST ratio should be inversely related to students' learning attainments as a teacher may have to concentrate on a small group of students. The results however, show that while this expectation holds

TABLE 4.4: Relationship Between Student-Teacher Ratio and Degree of Excellence (Faculty of Arts and Social Sciences)

ST Ratio	Excellance (% of Total Passed in Ist Division)		
	Low (< 50)	Medium (16-25)	High (26 >)
1	2	3	4
Low (<10)	Kerala, Panjab, Kurukshetra, Madras	—	Annamalai
Medium (10-15)	Gauhati, Mysore	—	—
High (15>)	—	Delhi, H.S. Gaur Bombay	—

true for one university namely Annamalai, in the cases of four other universities, namely, Kerala, Panjab, Kurukshetra and Madras such expectatioins are belied. The evidence, thus, show a mixed trend or relationship.

The results for the Faculty of Sciences, in Table 4.5 and Table 4.6, reveal almost a similar pattern, as discussed above, except that the ratios of first divisioners to the total pass-out students is much higher for most universities though the inter-university differences are glaring in terms of both unit costs as well as examination results. Whereas the universities of Annamalai and HS Gaur have emerged with high performance rates (and least costs), the universities of Banaras, Madras, Mysore and Panjab have emerged with low performance (and high costs). In other words, the universities in the former category are highly cost-effective as compared to those in the latter category. Another category of universities are those which fall in the high range of unit costs but they also maintained high performance rates. The universities in this category are Bombay, Delhi, Kerala, Kurukshetra and Utkal. These observations are, thus, consistent with those already made in the context of Faculty of Arts and Social Sciences.

The performance of the universities with respect to Faculty of Commerce and Management (Table 4.7), are self-evident; the results are therefore not discussed here.

4.3 Discipline-wise Results

In order to obtain a better insight into the aspects of efficiency in performance of universities, an attempt was also made to analyse the examination results at the disaggregated level i.e. by the major disciplines. The disciplines considered with respect to the Faculty of Arts and Social Sciences are: Economics, English, Hindi, History, Music, Political Science, Psychology, Sanskrit, Sociology (Table 4.8). The major subjects covered under the Faculty of Sciences are: Botany, Chemistry, Geography, Geology, Mathematics, Physics, Statistics and Zoology (Table 4.9). The major conclusions which emerge from the analysis of Tables 4.8 and 4.9 are:

First, inter-university and intra-university difference in the overall productivity as measured by pass-out rates are very wide. Some universities have consistently shown comparatively better results for most faculties and subjects of studies than others in the

TABLE 4.5: Relationship Between Student-Teacher Ratio and Unit Costs (Faculty of Sciences)

S. No.	University	Percentage of students appeared				Ist Div as % of Total Pass Out	STR	Unit Costs (in Rs.)
		Ist Div. %	IInd Div %	IIIrd Div %	Total Pass Out %			
1	2	3	4	5	6	7	8	9
1	Annamalai	61.3	14.0	—	75.3	81.4	11	4280
2	BHU	NA	NA	NA	21.4	NA	9	25048
3	Bombay	44.6	16.8	32.4*	93.8	47.5	11	17046
4	Delhi	57.2	26.1	8.2	91.5	62.5	8	15032
5	Gauhati	8.4	43.9	13.7	66.0	12.8	5	13036
6	HS Gaur	18.9	44.6	21.6	85.1	22.2	20	5043
7	Kerala	39.1	20.1	16.8	76.0*	5.15	7	24123
8	Kurukshetra	37.0	33.0	9.3	79.3	46.6	5	24695
9	Madras	22.7	9.0	6.8	38.5	58.9	6	23998
10	Mysore	10.7	10.9	23.9	45.5*	23.3	6	10759
11	Panjab	23.0	11.8	7.7	42.5*	54.0	5	24367
12	Utkal	NA	NA	NA	96.4	NA	5	19423

Note: Percentages have been calculated from the No. of Students appeared in the examination.

NA — Not Available.

* Includes Students Passed without Division.

Source: Computed from the relevant data contained in the Annual Reports 1988-89 of each university.

TABLE 4.6: Relationship Between Unit Costs and Students' Performance (Faculty of Sciences)

Costs Range (in Rs.)	Students' Performance (in %)		
	Low (< 50)	Medium (51-70)	High (71 >)
1	2	3	4
Low (<6000)	—	—	Annamalai, H.S. Gaur
Medium (6001 to 10000)	—	—	—
High (10000>)	BHU, Madras, Mysore, Panjab	Gauhati	Bombay, Delhi, Kerala, Kurukshetra, Utkal

sample. No attempt has, however, been made to rank them in terms of the level of performance, mainly because of inadequacy of relevant data for judging the overall productivity of a university or to determine the relationship between inputs and outputs of university activities. It must, however, be stressed that aggregate picture for the entire university system, and for the select universities examined above, conclusively indicate that a high rate of wastage that occur, inspite of low ST ratios and high unit costs, calls for a thorough scrutiny of the management of university resources. The indicators of performance, even at the departmental levels, corroborate the observations made at the institutional and faculty levels and demonstrate that the cause and effect relationship between inputs and outputs variables are not clearly discernible. Hence, the need for the further probing into the areas that affect productivity of university system.

Second, except in science disciplines, the share of students passing with sixty per cent or above marks is awfully low; which obviously, show a very low level of students' learning achievements. It therefore emerges that pursuits of excellence in higher education at most university centres are generally neglected, particularly in arts and social science disciplines. The fact that most universities have a very low ST ratio and some of them have been incurring higher unit costs as compared to other institutions, indicate that there may be

TABLE 4.7: Students' Performance, Student-Teacher Ratio and Unit Costs (Faculty of Commerce and Management)

S. No.	University	Ist Div. %	IInd Div %	IIIrd Div %	Total Pass Out	Ist Div as % of Total Pass Out	STR	Unit Costs (in Rs.)
1	2	3	4	5	6	7	8	9
1	Annamalai	38.3	44.7	NA	83.0	46.2	30	1540
2	Delhi	23.7	14.1	44.1	81.9	28.9	34	5614
3	HS Gaur	18.6	60.1	15.3	94.0	19.8	46	2478
4	Kurukshetra	7.1	39.6	39.5	86.2	8.2	6	19775
5	Madras	15.4	18.4	16.6	50.4	30.5	20	42016
6	Mysore	1.9	5.5	14.4	21.8	8.8	11	4979
7	Panjab	19.2	13.5	29.9	62.6	30.7	8	11966

Note: Percentage have been calculated from the No. of students appeared in the examination.

NA — Not available

* Includes Students Passed without Division

STR — Student Teacher Ratio

Source: Computed from the relevant data contained in the Annual Report 1988-89 of each university.

TABLE 4.8: Discipline-wise Students' Performance, Student-Teacher Ratio and Unit Costs (Faculty of Arts)

S. No.	University	Ist Div. %	IInd Div %	IIIrd Div %	Total Pass Out %	Ist Div as % of Total Pass Out	STR	Unit Costs (in Rs.)
1	2	3	4	5	6	7	8	9
ECONOMICS								
1	Annamalai	22.9	62.9	NA	85.0	26.7	15	5463
2	Bombay	8.9	34.8	36.3	80.0	11.1	28	5832
3	Gauhati	1.7	65.0	NA	66.7	2.6	20	4647
4	Kerala	1.2	9.9	34.6	42.7	2.8	12	6676
5	Panjab	3.0	16.8	28.6	48.7	6.2	13	8795
6	Kurukshetra	4.9	34.0	18.7	56.6	8.5	9	8195
ENGLISH								
1	Annamalai	14.3	76.2	NA	90.5	15.8	6	18554
2	Bombay	12.1	50.0	19.0	81.1	14.9	50	2769
3	Gauhati	NA	59.6	NA	59.6	NA	23	4580
4	Kerala	0.6	4.6	16.3	21.5	2.9	11	9964
5	Kurukshetra	1.6	24.5	14.2	40.3	4.0	17	6463
6	Panjab	0.5	21.4	41.8	63.7	0.8	14	8943

(Contd.)

TABLE 4.8 *(Contd.)*

1	2	3	4	5	6	7	8	9
HINDI								
1	Bombay	25.3	50.0	22.1	97.9	25.8	51	1563
2	Gauhati	4.8	71.4	NA	76.2	6.3	6	15314
3	Kerala	11.3	48.6	34.6	94.5	12.0	NA	NA
4	Kurukshetra	2.0	19.6	8.9	30.5	6.6	18	4698
5	Panjab	2.1	35.1	33.2	70.4	3.0	29	4733
HISTORY								
1	Annamalai	54.2	40.0	NA	94.2	57.6	13	7301
2	Bombay	13.5	57.7	15.4	86.6	15.6	29	4291
3	Gauhati	6.5	81.7	NA	88.2	7.3	22	4774
4	Kerala	1.2	6.7	32.8	40.6	2.9	14	10173
5	Kurukshetra	1.6	23.6	11.0	36.2	4.3	6	10516
6	Panjab	1.4	19.4	42.1	76.9	1.8	11	8791
MUSIC								
1	Bombay	40.0	40.0	20.0	100.0	40.0	51	4418
2	Kerala	10.5	52.6	15.8	78.9	13.3	NA	NA

(Contd.)

TABLE 4.8 *(Contd.)*

1	2	3	4	5	6	7	8	9
3	Kurukshetra	46.4	42.9	3.6	92.9	50.0	11	7734
4	Panjab	37.1	45.7	12.9	95.7	39.4	6	15800
POL. SCIENCE								
1	Annamalai	42.1	5.3	47.4	94.8	44.4	7	8950
2	Gauhati	1.4	17.9	NA	73.3	1.9	33	2394
3	Kerala	5.3	31.4	36.1	72.8	7.3	7	10144
4	Kurukshetra	6.2	25.7	45.4	71.3	0.3	10	8948
PSYCHOLOGY								
1	Annamalai	38.5	30.8	NA	69.3	55.6	5	20095
2	Bombay	13.2	34.2	34.2	81.6	16.1	40	4432
3	Kerala	50.0	45.0	5.0	100.0	50.0	6	13750
4	Kurukshetra	28.0	40.0	4.0	72.0	38.9	5	11670
SANSKRIT								
1	Annamalai	NA	33.3	33.3	66.6	NA	24	27000
2	Delhi	16.7	66.7	NA	83.4	20.0	4	29545

(Contd.)

TABLE 4.8 (Contd.)

1	2	3	4	5	6	7	8	9
3	Kurukshetra	24.4	37.8	28.9	91.1	26.8	7	3590
4	Madras	30.4	26.8	1.8	59.0	20.0	4	14878
5	Mysore	19.7	44.3	21.3	85.3	23.1	3	14324
SOCIOLOGY								
1	Annamalai	16.7	83.3	NA	100.0	16.7	11	4496
2	Bombay	14.6	26.8	41.5	82.9	17.6	30	5286
3	Kerala	NA	7.0	27.4	34.4	NA	10	17184

Note : Percentage have been calculated from the No. of students appeared in the examinations.

NA — Not available

Source: Examination results have been computed from the Annual Report 1988-89 of each University.

TABLE 4.9: Discipline-wise Students' Performance, Student-Teacher Ratio and Unit Costs (Faculty of Science)

S. No.	University	Ist Div. %	IInd Div %	IIIrd Div %	Total Pass Out %	Ist Div as % of Total Pass Out	STR	Unit Costs (in Rs.)
1	2	3	4	5	6	7	8	9
BOTANY								
1	Annamalai	76.8	8.9	NA	85.7	89.7	13	5773
2	Gauhati	51.9	45.5	NA	97.4	53.3	6	16595
3	Kerala	51.7	28.0	12.7	92.4	56.0	3	30445
4	Kurukshetra	88.9	5.6	NA	94.5	94.1	4	15834
5	Panjab	NA	NA	NA	61.1	NA	12	19738
CHEMISTRY								
1	Annamalai	32.8	NA	NA	32.8	100.0	9	9207
2	Bombay	64.7	35.3	NA	100.0	64.7	10	15759
3	Gauhati	49.0	26.5	NA	75.5	64.9	5	26881
4	Kerala	44.3	13.6	3.4	61.3	72.2	7	12620
5	Kurukshetra	73.8	4.8	NA	78.6	93.9	4	20731

(Contd.)

TABLE 4.9 *(Contd.)*

1	2	3	4	5	6	7	8	9
GEOGRAPHY								
1	Gauhati	17.3	81.3	NA	98.7	17.6	9	13015
2	Kerala	33.3	66.7	NA	100.0	33.3	6	7320
3	Kurukshetra	21.8	58.2	10.9	90.9	24.0	10	8202
MATHEMATICS								
1	Annamalai	59.5	18.9	NA	78.4	75.9	13	5308
2	Bombay	40.0	30.0	23.3	93.3	42.0	14	7190
3	Gauhati	17.4	51.3	NA	68.7	25.3	14	6216
4	Kerala	51.9	16.0	18.9	86.8	59.8	8	7314
5	Kurukshetra	29.3	12.2	2.4	43.9	66.7	9	6943
PHYSICS								
1	Annamalai	65.7	NA	NA	65.7	100.0	15	5774
2	Bombay	58.6	34.5	NA	93.1	63.0	9	1716
3	Gauhati	32.8	44.3	NA	77.1	42.5	6	20688
4	Kerala	86.7	13.3	NA	100.0	86.7	11	9384
5	Kurukshetra	90.6	NA	NA	90.6	100.0	5	17571

(Contd.)

TABLE 4.9 *(Contd.)*

1	2	3	4	5	6	7	8	9
STATISTICS								
1	Annamalai	36.4	18.2	NA	54.6	66.7	9	6688
2	Bombay	59.5	33.3	7.1	95.9	62.5	15	5734
3	Gauhati	13.8	67.7	NA	73.5	18.8	3	23313
4	Kurukshetra	42.6	37.5	NA	78.1	52.0	6	10423
ZOOLOGY								
1	Annamalai	62.2	25.6	NA	87.8	70.9	21	4054
2	Gauhati	46.6	50.7	NA	97.3	47.9	7	14210

Note: Percentage have been calculated from the No. of students appeared in the examinations.

Source: Examination results have been computed from the Annual Report 1988-89 of each University.

NA — Not Available.

some other factors, than physical and financial inputs, affecting the academic achievements. If so, factors need to be identified for appropriate policy decisions.

Even in important disciplines like economics, political science and sociology, for instance, the proportion of students passing with more than 60 per cent marks has varied between 2 to 10 per cent of the total pass-out students, which indicate low standards of higher education in these disciplines. The picture is no different for language subjects either, particularly, Hindi and English. In science disciplines, pass-out rates are generally very high, though there are university to university differences. A significant majority of students in sciences pass with over 60 per cent marks, which, unlike the subjects in arts and social sciences, show encouraging results. This is however partly attributable *inter-alia* to high unit costs and low ST ratios, as compared of courses of non-science subjects.

Third, in absence of the detailed information about the students' profile particularly the scores at the previous examinations, some measure of the environment for teaching and learning including collaborative efforts made by various levels of university functionaries, the quality of students' support services that facilitate students academic attainments, and the tools used for assessing students' performance, etc., it is difficult to pin-point the factors, and the extent to which they could be said to be, responsible for influency the efficiency of unversity system. The comparability of cost-effectiveness is also marred somewhat by such factors as the difference in admission criteria, infrastructure facilities and level of funding by the Centre and the States. Inspite of the given limitations; such as these, the comparisions of unit costs vis-a-vis the examination scores by disciplines, attempted above, lend desirable perspective about the relative cost-effectiveness of the programme carried out by different universities.

4.4 Concluding Remarks

Finally, there is much to be desired in so far as internal and external efficiency of university system are concerned. The analysis of unit costs revealed considerable mis-allocation of funds as evident from wide variations in per student costs. This demonstrates internal inefficiency of the system in making judicious use of resources. Likewise, high wastage rate together with the low degree of performance in pursuing the goals of promoting excellence in higher education are the indication of low external efficiency of the system since the economic value of university outputs is inherently low. These together affect the overall productivity of the education system as well as other sectors of development, which benefit from network educational activities. In effect, thus, there is the case for enhancing cost-effectiveness of the university system with a view to both justifying the levels of investments that are being made in the prevailing regime of 'resource crunch' as well as improving its credibility to attract funds from the Government and other sources to finance high quality of relevant teaching, research and training programmes to effectively promote the objective of human resource development.

FIVE

POLICY INFERENCES

This study has primarily focussed on the assessment of efficiency of university system in India. In examining the question of efficiency, the following aspects have been analysed. First, the policies and patterns of allocation of resources by the funding agencies to different types of universities have been examind, particularly in the context of a select number of well established universities in different parts of the country. Second, the distribution of funds by universities for various educational purposes and that under different heads of expenditure have been analysed in absolute and relative terms to reflect both the patterns of utilisation of funds and the extent to which universities differ from one another in prioritisation of programmes for funding. Third, with a view to assessing internal efficiency of universities, especially in terms of judicious use of funds, on comparative basis, the unit costs (per student) exercises have been undertaken to demonstrate the degree of economic use of resources for realising the comparable objectives of promotion of teaching and research in various disciplines. Fourth, in order that some idea is gained about external efficiency of the university system, students' performance in relation to crucial inputs like per student costs and student-teacher ratios, which are the major determinants of quality of teaching, have been examined. The relevant comparisions reveal *inter-alia* the degree of efforts made, and level of achievement, in pursuing the goal of 'excellence' in higher education. Besides, it reveals the extent of wastages as measured by failures in examinations or mis-allocation of resources. In the light of the major findings of study and the observations made in the preceding Chapters, the significant implications for policy formulation are discussed below.

5.1 The Policy and Pattern of Funding

The universities in India are largely financed by the Government—the

Centre and the States. While differences in financial dependence of universities *inter-se* are glaring, the Central universities financed through the University Grants Commission (UGC) are relatively more dependent and better off as well than the State universities, which constitute a majority and enrol more than 90 per cent of students in higher education. Of the various causes of variations in relative dependence of universities, the differences in financial capacities of different levels of Governments i.e. the Centre vis-a-vis the States and lack of uniform approach of funding are most dominant ones. Under the existing arrangement of funding higher education institutions by the Centre and States, the universities are largely financed by the States which are indeed at various stages of economic development. The extent of support provided by them naturally differs due to their relative fiscal capacities as assessed by per capita income of the States and priorities assigned to development programme which are naturally oriented towards meeting the minimum human needs for a decent standard of living. Lack of adequate positive intervention by the Centre to nullify the States fiscal deficiencies, arising mainly from income constraints, in augmenting resources for higher education and, or the lack of States own endeavors to rationalize the approach of determination of a university's eligibility for funds on the basis of realistic requirements, considerable degrere of mis-allocation of resources occur in the university system. This is evident from the fact that the magnitude of physical and financial inputs, on the one hand, and the qualitative and quantitative levels of educational outputs on the other, obviously for the comparable programmes, differ so widely. This is also true for Central universities financed by the UGC.

It emerges, therefore, that the existing resource allocation policy for the development of higher education is inefficient and inequitous as well, since the approaches of distribution of funds by the Centre (read UGC) and the States are not suitably matched with the financial requirements of the programmes of higher education. The inter-university variations in unit costs are unjustifiably too high. It can also be said that the mechanisms of funding in vogue hardly allows for ensuring financial accountability of universities. Not only patterns of allocation of funds among the universities are inequitable but the earmarking of resources to different academic departments and units of common services by the universities themselves are quite haphazard both in relative and absolute terms. The allocation pattern, therefore, bear no relationship with the types and levels of educational activities, which is attributable to lack of effective planning of educational services either at the national or the States or the university levels. The issue that emanate from these observations is: how to minimise mis-allocation of resources, which results in either under investment leading to qualitative deterioration or excess expenditure resulting in diseconomies of university programmes.

It seems desirable that a uniform approach of funding of all the comparable programmes/disciplines, which are carried out by the universities and colleges in the country should be adopted by a nodal agency like UGC for the following reasons: (i) the national policies have laid emphasis on balanced regional development through the enrichment of human resources, in which education and training play a crucial role, (ii) the degrees/diplomas awarded by all the institutions are theoretically treated at par throughout the country, and (iii) the funds are provided to the universities from the Central pool of resources, irrespective of the channels adopted by the Centre and the states for devolution of resources. In view of these and many more advantages as discussed later, the mechanism of funding ought not create any differences in the levels of investments in human resources, particularly at the inputs stage by allocating different sizes of funds for comparable teaching and research programmes. The steps towards rationalization of funding of higher education would necessitate *inter alia* the following for ensuring equilization of educational opportunities among different federating states, institutions and socio-economic groups.

First, the allocation of funds to each university department should be made on the basis of unit costs, the determination of which should take into account the positive as well as normative considerations to ensure adequate level of funding with a view to maintaining reasonable standard of education throughout the country. The approach of funding in vogue, mainly on non-plan basis, does not allow for weeding out of sub-standard or irrelevant programmes. This therefore calls for continuous monitoring and evaluation of each programme at different university centres for suitable modifications and, more importantly, within the framework of perspective educational plan of national development. Funds should accordingly be provided on the basis of realistic requirements which should be worked out by employing both the approach of unit costs as obtaining to the average extent for a group of well established institutions of higher education as well as the sound judgement of financial needs to ensure high standard of various schemes.

As regards the new schemes, the existing practice of financing plan expenditure by the Centre, the States and the UGC on 100 per cent basis to some institutions and on matching basis to some others, is unscientific as it creates inequity and inefficiency in management of institutions. Needless to mention, differences in the institutional abilities to produce requisite manpower adversely affect the level of skills formation, extent of innovation and use of technological know-how in productive activities. This, in turn, impinge upon the efforts to improve the quality of life of people. Therefore, the new educational schemes which are envisaged to effectively meet the challenges of development, in the short and the long-run, should be managed-financially and administratively—by the nodal agencies in consultation with all the related departments so that the schemes should be successfully launched and implemented to yield the desirable results. At present, such development schemes get hampered due to sharing of plan expenditure on matching basis between the Centre and the States, which differ a great deal insofar as their plan priorities and fiscal capacities to finance various programmes are concerned; particularly when the burden of financing the programmes finally devolves on the States, after the expiry of plan period. As a result of this, in the present allocation mechanism, the limited plan funds get either thinly distributed across the institutions throughout the country or the institutions mainly those from the advanced States, which are able to contribute to matching portions, are able to attract more funds than others from the Centre (i.e. UGC). Such an approach not only adversely affect the quality of relevant programmes but jeoparadizes the efforts to uniformly promote human resource development through education across the federating States.

In view of this, an integrated approach of financing plan and non-plan schemes needs to be evolved by taking advantage of unit costs analysis for planning and management of resources. The funds should be made available on realistic assessment of requirements of the programmes carried out by different universities and colleges. Without ensuring adequate level of investment in education across the institutions/regions, it is not possible to uniformly raise and maintain high standard of education which is a precondition for social development and economic growth.

Second, resources are limited and the pressure of demand for higher education, mainly from unmotivated students, is very high. In order that meagre funds are judiciously deployed among the institutions to attain and maintain the stipulated degree of standard of education, it would be necessary to plan the number of students for various types and levels of courses offered by the institutions for the purposes of financing teaching programmes. The Government funds should be restricted to the planned number which should be determined on the basis of sound assessment of manpower requirements of economy and other social considerations to ensure representation of various sections of society in different socio-economic activities of the country. Of the total pre-determined planned number of students, each institution should be indicated the number of students at each level and for each programme. The share of an institution in the total planned number of students should be determined on the basis of performance in teaching and research, at least to the national average extent, and accordingly government funding should be assured. The eligibility for grants of each institution with respect to each programme should be determined separately and the gross total grants for all the disciplines, when pooled together, should constitute the block grant for teaching functions.

If an institution enrols more students than already indicated to it for the Government support, it would do so as an autonomous organisation with its own resources or at the risk of diluting the quality of education, in which case the level of funding in the future would be adversely affected due to deterioration in standard of teaching and subsequent reduction in allocation of planned number of students for funding purposes in the foreseable future.

Needless to mention, the institutions enrolling students from educationally backward regions and communities should be given special treatment to enable them to meet the costs of providing special services to upgrade educational levels of students from deprived groups. The requirements of such institutions on account of educational services to backward communities should obviously be worked out in relation to the need to cope with the challenge of meeting qualitative and quantitative dimensions of problems of educationally backward communities or regions.

Third, the research activities at most universities are at a low ebb because of either inadequate infrastructure or lack of competent staff or both. The university documents namely Annual Budget/

Annual Reports hardly present separate data on physical and financial allocation for research development, which pose difficulties in making quantitative assessment of research efforts. Since teaching and research are tightly related, research programmes should be duly vitalized by making separate funding arrangements. The policy of funding research at university centres should be formulated such that quality research in different disciplines could be promoted without unduly sacrificing the need to improve the relevance of research inputs for productivity gains. The policy on funding research schemes should be so designed that university departments could attract sufficient funds from the Government and commercial organisations for building infrastructure for not only high standards of research outputs in theoretical and applied fields but also for effective teaching and training programmes.

The major advantages of adopting a uniform approach of funding higher education based on realistic requirements for the planned number of students, as discussed above, would be as under:

(a) Inefficiency in functioning of universities due to mis-allocation of resources by different funding agencies of the Centre and the States would be minimized. The new approach of funding would duly introduce elements of competition among the institutions to bid for limited government funds and the institutions having better academic performance as judged from efficient utilization of resources and students' learning attainments would attract more funds than others.

(b) Inter-university differences in unit costs of comparable educational programmes would be narrowed. In the process some savings would be realized in the institutions where unit costs are high. Alternatively, due to resource equilisation efficiency would be improved, in the institutions suffering from inadequacy of funds.

(c) The process of educational planning especially with regard to manpower requirements of emerging industrial economy could be made more effective. In the new approach, the financial instruments could be used for both to control or regulate the activities of institutions which are producing unemployable graduates (or not desirably cost-effective) as well as to motivate the students and institutions to participate in the educational programmes that have direct bearing on creation of wealth of the country. In effect, thus, the uniform approach of funding based on realistic requirements for planned students would create conducive conditions for a meaningful physical and financial planning to manage the educational system.

Finally, the priority areas of research in theoretical and applied fields would duly get promoted thorough a separate policy for funding research in the university sector. As teaching and research are tightly related, promotion of research in universities is *sine quo non* for effective teaching and learning. As discussed above, the new mechanism of funding would duly ensure promotion of higher education among deprived groups for equity reasons. Also the high costs programmes in the fields of science and technology would get financed on requirement basis, which would ensure efficiency and usefulness of such courses.

5.2 Improving Cost-Efficiency

The evidences pertaining to unit costs analysis and the degree of students' learning attainments showed divergent trends for different universities even with respect to comparable programmes. In other words, the cost functions which denote relationship between inputs and outputs differ due to the factors that are both internal and external to the system. In fact, the factors like demand for higher education, Governments' financial support, utilization of funds and effectiveness of teaching-learning process are influenced by numerous factors relating to socio-economic and political considerations which are not easily amenable to quantitative analysis. It is therefore difficult to isolate the factors and measure the extent to which each of them are responsible for determining the shape and nature of cost functions in different universities. The comparisons of unit costs of various academic and non-academic services duly prove the point and demonstrate that relative degree of influence of each factor or head of expenditure varies so widely that it becomes difficult to indicate the areas and extent of reduction in per student costs. It is, therefore, for the universities themselves to (a) ascertain whether or not they are able to ensure reasonable degree of cost-efficiency which obviously takes into account both the financial inputs for each package of the programme and the quality and quantity of outputs; and (b) compare these results with those of other universities which are providing comparable services. The approach of analysis in which unit costs have been compared with the students' performance, as demonstrated in this study, should be taken as tentatively suggestive for further investigations. As against this backdrop, the following major areas for improving efficiency in use of resources are indicated.

First, the practice of budgeting resources for various university programmes ought to be modified such as to reflect a greater degree of transparency in the amount of expenditure incurred on each package of programme for different purposes on the one hand and the qualitative and quantitative attainments on the other. The existing practice of presenting physical and financial data hardly allows for making objective analysis of finances of universities in relation to their performance. In essence, the deployment of physical and financial resources should duly allow for undertaking cost-effectiveness analysis. Such an analysis would considerably improve the planning and management of resources through continuous monitoring and evaluation of on-going programmes; and for the future, some feedback would be obtained for improving cost-efficiency of university system. The cost-effectiveness analysis undertaken in this study indicate, in general, that most universities could improve their performance with the existing level of funding, as there are university departments which spend much less yet their performance is highest and *vice-versa*.

Second, there ought to be valid justification or rationalization of needs for teaching and non-teaching staff and other infrastructure facilities for a given level and type of programme. In view of specific objectives and the geo-cultural environment in which a university has to function, the requirements should be objectively determined to adequately cater for the manpower requirements of the region. It may be said without prevarication that inter-university and intra-university difference indicate ample scope for (i) reducing the already high level of expenditure on certain heads of expenditure, mainly of non-academic nature comprising payment of salaries to non-teaching staff and maintenance of administrative units; and (ii) improving the effectiveness of teaching-learning process by ensuring efficient use of the existing level of physical facilities since student-teacher ratios in most university departments have been estimated to be favourably very low and in many institutions infrastructure like labs, library classrooms, etc. are not fully utilized. It is quite probable that high quality of relevant programmes could be supported in some departments by raising the level of financial allocation. The results of our exercises discussed in the preceding chapters provide cue for an incisive probe with respect to each university and the heads of expenditure that require a close security for improving internal financial management.

Third, the activities like conduct of examinations and completion of formalities like admissions by each university consumes a large share of an already meagre resources allocated for the development of higher education. It would be worthwhile for the universities to co-operate and coordinate activities, at least in the fields of common concern and introduce the system of common entrance test as IITs, IIMs and other medical institutes do in this country. Similarly, the affiliating universities, which have a major responsibility of conducting examinations should be absolved of this responsibility and the tasks of conducting examination could be entruested to a nodal agency. Apart from ensuring uniformity in admission criteria and standards of education, the approach suggested above would generate significant economies of scale or improve overall cost efficiency in management of universities. The savings thus generated could be ploughed back for reinvestment on socially useful and economically productive higher education programmes.

Finally, most universities cater to educational needs in the fields of general higher education i.e. in the areas of Humanities, Arts and Social Sciences. The emergence of distance learning system supported by the advanced communication technologies allow for shifting the burden of the conventional system of education towards distance learning modes, which have significant potential to provide higher education at the least cost, apart from ensuring equality of opportunity and effectiveness of programmes. In cooperation with the distance learning institutes, conventional universities could promote higher education and, at the same time, the latter, in turn, would get its financial burden alleviated by shifting the enrolment burden on distance learning institution which are better able to promote teaching-learning process in the fields of general higher education, which constitute nearly 65 per cent of the total enrolment. A concerted effort in this direction would surely improve overall cost-efficiency of the university system.

5.3 Fiscal Instruments for Ensuring Cost-Effectiveness

The policy of pricing and/or subsidizing higher education can be effectively used for ensuring cost-effectiveness of various programmes carried out by the universities. Specifically, the following instruments of resource mobilization should be regularly reviewed in relations to the costs of educational services to augment adequate resources as well as to effect desirable changes in quality of relevant programmes.

Firstly, the share of tuition fee in the total costs of education is very low and falls in the range of one to five per cent. Inspite of manifold increase in tuition fee by a number of universities in the recent past, requirements of universities being too high are not likely to be sufficiently provided for to enable them to cope with the challenges of higher education. Yet, a beginning already made in this direction is most welcome to recover the costs from beneficiary groups who are largely drawn from better off sections of the society. Since the costs of education vary across the institutions and programmes of learning, the rate of tuition fee should be fixed in relations to the costs of programme which should be borne by students out of their incomes or of their parents or loans/grants obtained for the purpose from the specific institutions established for providing educational loans. Since higher education in its major part constitute investment in human resource development, the Government should clearly outline its policy of financing social sectors like education and health while ensuring equity and efficiency in the provision of essential services. What is being suggested here is that tuition fee should be enhanced substantially and students financial capacities should also be duly strengthened by providing loans/grants on merit-cum-means basis; in which case government policy of subsidizing higher education should be directly oriented towards students, rather than institutions which indiscriminately extend the benefits of subsidy to students, mainly in favour of those drawn from the better off sections. Another obvious advantage of this approach would be that the students' community or their parents would be genuinely concerned about the package of educational programmes offered by institutions and they would therefore emerge as a vocal group to demand for high quality of relevant programmes, since they would have to pay for their wards' education either from their current or future incomes. In any case, cost-effectiveness would improve without unduly burdening the economy or changing the priorities of development.

Secondly, the total recoveries from students comes to 15 to 20 per cent of the institutional costs and most affiliating universities are able to do it through the major activities like conduct of examinations and distance education programmes which allow them to generate surpluses for financing the general programme of the universities. The fact is that the clientele groups who join a majority of non-viable colleges, undertake examinations as regular or non-collegiate students or those who join distance learning institutions as deprived groups, are generally drawn from less privileged families. Obviously, then, such modes of collection of revenues to further subsidize the education of other fellow learners from a relatively better-off sections are highly unethical and inequitious inso far as the policy of financing educational services is concerned. Likewise, the rates of various user's charges like hostel, lab, library fees, etc., need to be objectively determined and recovered. And the revenues thus raised should be re-invested for improving the student support services, rather than sacrificing the quality of services.

Thirdly, the education of foreign students should not be subsidised to the extent being done today. The recoveries from foreign students in US dollars would meet the much needed resources for import of educational technologies, modernization of curricula and facilities in the university sector. For instance, there are over 13 thousand foreign students in India. If an amount of 300 US dollars per student is charged to recover a part of the cost of education, the total collection of about 40 thousand US dollars (or about Rs. 12 crores) would be sufficient enough to run a university in India. A few universities have recently begun to charge foreign students in US dollars. The remaining universities too should charge full costs of education to pay for the bill on account of imports of educational aids including equipment, books and journals, which have become so costly that Indian universities can hardly afford to buy them.

Fourthly, a concerted effort is required to be made to raise resources from non-traditional sources such as industry and other commercial concerns, which are making use of highly qualified and trained manpower produced by the institutions of higher learning. Such an effort especially by technical and professional institutions would greatly reduce the present financial burden on the Central and the State governments. The relevant laws provide for 125 per cent exemption from Income Tax for donations to universities/institutions. These institutions ought to devise ways and means of attracting funds from industry while the UGC should provide for minimum infrastructure facilities for training and research which are pre-requisites for industrial funding through consultancy schemes. The funds from industries and other business houses could be tapped by (a) introducing such courses of studies and training programmes that are relevant to the manpower needs of industries for increasing productivity; and (b) undertaking consultancy research projects, the findings of which would be conducive in reorienting the industrial sector for reducing costs of production and increasing its profitability. Moreover, the public and private sector enterprises should be encouraged to sponsor a specified number of students especially in technical and professional fields, whom they can employ after their graduation. Such an approach would considerably reduce the financial burden of the government while the relevance of education and training would naturally improve due to the programme linked sponsorship. The institutes of higher learning should however strengthen themselves by way of improving infrastructure, modifying and raising the level of their academic expertise in the applied areas to attract industrial funding, while the industry should be encouraged, by providing fiscal incentives, to sponsor the programmes relevant to their needs. The culture of industrial funding of higher education and research ought to be promoted in the interst of improving overall productivity as signalled by the current on-going economic reforms.

It must also be pointed out in passing that the conventional system of education should tap the opportunities now thrown open to them in the new schemes of libralised economy. A number of privately managed institutions have come up overtime and they are providing market oriented courses of varying durations for fresh graduates as well as to those who are already employed and would like to improve their knowledge and skills. The courses are offered on self-financing basis. But there are not many institutions fully or partly funded by the government, which have come forward to offer vocational programmes for graduates. As the competition between the institutions grows overtime, it might become too late for conventional institutions of higher education to enter into the market of supply of educated and trained manpower. In fact, the ability of institutions to successfully launch and carry out the socially useful and economically relevant programmes would determine their contributions to national development, which, in effect, influence the social financial support for its sustenance.

Fifthly, with a view to ploughing back the investments that are being made in every plan, appropriate mechanism needs to be evolved for administering the scheme of inflationary adjusted interest-free loans so as to improve the ability of students to pay for the package of education offered, of their choice, by the institutions. The collection of revenues, thus raised, should be used to expand the facilities for higher education. Under such a system, financial assistance should be made available from public funds in the forms of loan on merit-cum-means basis as mentioned earlier. Such assistance should be provided on the condition that they enter into a contract to repay the loan without interest after they begin to earn. The payment schedule should be spread over the average earning span of life. For providing such loans, the criteria of determining eligibility for loans should duly take into account such factors as academic standards, parental income and manpower requirements in specialised disciplines. The management of educational loans should be entrusted to an autonomous financial body which may be named as 'Educational Opportunity Bank' established on the pattern of Housing Development Bank. While such a scheme would ensure recovery of investments in higher education, the financial accountability on the part of both the students and the institutions would duly increase. It must be reiterated that loosing sight of cost-effectiveness of higher education programmes would not serve the purpose of either equity or human resource development.

Sixthly, the approach of funding of higher education through industry and specific financial institutions as pointed out above would essentially pave the way for an explicit and greater degree of privatisation or self-financing of university programmes. The fact that a large number of university level institutions includng colleges and most of the primary and secondary schools where the children of better off sections receive education do not get financial assistance from the Government, there is no reason why the financing of higher education cannot be made fuly transparent even when equity and efficiency consideration demand so. Furthermore, more than 11.5 per cent of the total enrolment in higher education is in open learning institutions and their education is largely self-financed even though such institutions are supposed to cater for deprived groups of students. The question therefore, is why cannot we gradually adopt an open policy of self-financing of higher education atleast in professional category which is surely an investment, with sufficient safeguards, of course, to protect the interest of motivated learners? A number of universities from abroad are attracting Indian students from better off sections who willingly pay a higher price for quality education. Why such opportunities should not be given to institutions in India? A number of independent universities in Asia and Europe have been established and they are marketing educational programmes even in India. We too have similar practices which allows non-aided institutions to charge higher fees as prescribed by the Government, particularly for employment oriented programmes. The existing practices however lack desirable transparency and determination to transcribe policies into meaningful actions. What is important is to devise a sound funding mechanism by which a greater degree of financial autonomy could be assured to arrest the deteriorating quality and relevance of education lest the promotion of human resource development of reasonable standard should remain an elusive objective.

Finally, the decision of the UGC to abondon the practice of adjusting the block grants with the revenues collected by universities would go a long way in motivating the universities to attract funds from different sources and methods. Till recently, practice of providing block grants net of revenues collected from different sources had a dampening effect on the efforts and motivation of universities to raise resources from different sources and methods. In order that fiscal efforts and prudence of universities are appreciated and rewarded by every possible means, the State Governments too, like UGC, should allow the universities financed by them to retain the revenues collected by the universities' own efforts for reinvestment on the programmes of national and local importance.

In brief, the beneficiaries should pay according to their income abilities or meet the educational expenses out of the interest-free loans payable over the life span of earnings while the education of poor sections of society should be suitably subsidised by the Government. The financial dependence of universities on Government would be gradually reduced somewhat and so would get minimised the government interference in the university autonomy. In effect, the implementation of suggestions made above would lead to not only improving cost-effectiveness of university programmes but the responsiveness of higher education system to diverse nature of manpower requirements of the country would also duly increase, which are so crucial to the task of accelerating the pace of development.

BIBLIOGRAPHY

Alebrechet, D. and Z. Iderman, A. (1992) *Financing Universities in Developing Countries*, The World Bank.

Ansari, M.M. (1995) *Alternative Methods of Financing Education*, Asian Development Bank/IRD London, TA Project on HRD in FSM, Pohenpai.

—, (1997) *Resource Mobilisation by Universities*, Spellbound Publication Ltd.

—, (1987) *Education and Economic Development: Perspectives for Policy Planning*, Association of Indian Universities, New Delhi.

—, (1989) 'Financial Health of Universities: A Diagnostic Study, *Journal of Higher Education*, Vol. 14, pp. 65-66.

—, (1991) Industry-Universities in India: Is Collaborative Effort Succeeding, *Industry and Higher Education*, Sept. (with T.C. Sharma).

—, (1991) 'University Finances: Determinants and Implications' in *Higher Education in India* by Moonis Raza (Ed). AIU.

—, (1992) *Economics of Distance Higher Education*, Concept Publishing Company, New Delhi.

—, (1994), *Fiscal Policy for University Development*, Concept Publishing Company.

—, (1996), Education: An Exercise in Shadow Boxing, *Financial Express*.

Association of Indian Universities, (1992) *Financial Deficits in Universities*, New Delhi.

Azad, J.L., (1975) *Financing of Higher Education in India*, Sterling Publishers Pvt. Ltd., New Delhi.

—, (1991) *Graduate Unemployment in India*, AIU.

—, (1988) *Higher Education in India: The Deepening Financial Crisis*, Radiant Publishers, New Delhi.

Govt. of India (1992) *National Policy on Education*, MHRD, New Delhi.

—, (1948) *University Education Commission*, Ministry of Education, New Delhi.

—, (1966) *Education and National Development* (Education Commission), Ministry of Education, New Delhi.

—, (1985) *Challenge of Education: A Policy Perspective*, New Delhi.

Garg, V.P. (1985) *Cost Analysis in Higher Education*, Metropolitan, New Delhi.

Jimenez, Emmanuel (1987) *Pricing Policy in the Social Sectors: Cost Recovery for Education and Health in Developing Countries Baltimore*, John Hopking.

Psacharopoulos, G., (1973) *Return to Education: An International Comparison*, Jossey-Bass, Elsevier.

—, (1981) 'Returns to Education: An Updated International Comparison', *Comparative Education*, Vol. 17, No. 3.

Raza, Moonis (1991) *Higher Education in India*, AIU.

Salmi, Jamil (1991) *Perspectives on the Financing of Higher Education*, The World Bank, Document No. PHREE/91/45.

Schultz, Theodore W. (1971) *Investment in Human Copital: The Role of Education and Research*, Free, New York.

University Grants Commission (1993) *UGC Funding of Institutions of Higher Education*, Report of Justice Dr. K. Punnayya Committee, 1992-93.

Zeenat Begam (1989) 'Facility Utilisation in University Sector', *Yojna*, Nov. 1-15.

INDEX